Red Ink Behaviors

Measure the Surprisingly High Cost of Problem Behaviors in Valuable Employees

by Jean A. Hollands

Blake/Madsen Publishers, 1997

Red Ink Behaviors: Measure the Surprisingly High Cost of Problem Behaviors in Valuable Employees.

First Edition

ISBN 0-96579-0-7

Scans: Palmer's
              Mountain View, CA
              (415) 969-1950

Publisher: Blake/Madsen
              257 Bryant Ave.
              Mountain View, CA 94040

Table of Contents

How the hero turns into the goat: Certain working styles eventually go sour. About the disguises, the interventions, the backfires, the opportunities.

The Birth Of The Costimator. The Costimator Up Close And Personal. How To Figure Out Exactly How Much The Negative Behaviors Cost.

Examples Of People You Love To Hate...

Why Do These Behaviors Happen?

Chapter Four: Timely Interventions.......... 79
Why The Problem People Are The Last To Learn About It...

Chapter Five: Red Ink Into Black Ink Behaviors....................................... 87
Success Stories

*The Good News About Interventions. Beware of the
The Hesitation Step. How To Sleep Nights...*

Appendix

**WARNING: GLC PROGRAMS ARE ALSO
OFFERED TO BLACK INK HIGH POTENTIAL
EMPLOYEES WHO HAVE NO MAJOR FLAWS
AND SIMPLY NEED LEADERSHIP ENHANCE-
MENT PROGRAMS.**

Acknowledgments

GLC has a staff of twenty people who contributed to this work. No one escaped my zeal and passion and distress over this project. The staff all worked the costimator on themselves, their clients, and even their families, I imagine. We all believe in the formula. It's very nice to work in a setting where others are enthusiastic about the task. We also received help from professionals in the valley who were willing to risk trying on some numbers with us.

Teddi McDonald did the cover, page lay-outs and editing. My whole family and staff put up with me in the months of preparation for this launch. Joan Blake and Jeff Lugerner gave me special encouragement in dark hours.

Our President, Bill Paradis, worked very hard and was a key player in this drama. Thank you for your support. Jean Frederic Aboudarham also was a great help in developing the formula for this project.

Others who really encouraged me when my faith shook a little were Laura and Ron Steck, Dr. Pat Rice and Christina Syrett and of course, Helene Deigan. Robin and Todd Hollands, Krista Henley, Frank del Fiugo, Angela Leung, Nancy Whittlesey, Sandy Petersen, Valerie Goss, Mareca Hatler, Kathy Schlosser, Jeanne Butler and Paul and Liz Nyberg are always in my camp. It's done. Now we are ready.

INTRODUCTION:

John Brown, Vice President, Marketing, was committing professional suicide. It was hard to watch. Like taking a razor blade to his wrist, John slit his career with the reactionary stance he often took these days. He had become expensive to his company—far more expensive than his salary and benefits. Far more expensive than the technical brilliance he contributed to the project team. Far more expensive than the people around him deserved. Far more expensive than his company could calculate. After fourteen years with this blue chip organization, John was now beginning to cost the company almost a million dollars a year.

How do we know this? Well, we figured it out. Frankly, it was not so hard to figure it out theoretically. It was very hard, however, to digest the enormity of the numbers. My colleagues kept wanting to rub their white gloves over the numbers. Our technical people kept shaking their heads. I became alarmed. What awful black hole had we uncovered? Would people really believe how costly it is to have a difficult employee on board? Would they understand that one bad apple or one untrained leader can rupture a whole department, can cause morale decay and can cost enormous amounts of money?

I felt like we were discovering a new human virus. This flu is far reaching. The effects are endemic. It touches John's boss, his peers, their peers, his subordinates, their subordinates. It contaminates John's customers and the contracts with which his successful corporation is engaged. The illness also touches John. He knows that he is no longer effective, but he attempts to hide it, especially from himself. He frets in the middle of the night and he hides himself during the working day, behind a meaningless project, behind a business trip, behind the pointing of the finger of blame at others.

The kinds of problems we are talking about may be at work in your office too. Almost every company has someone whose value has diminished. They are employees who no longer contribute. They are too high maintenance for the boss or their colleagues. Or they are excellent employees who need new skills to match their new responsibilities. How many times have we talked about the brilliant scientists or engineers who are promoted but left floundering to lead or collaborate with the rest of the technical team? These employees contribute to the *red ink, not the black.* Their working styles or behaviors are a financial drain to the company.

For easy reference, we will tag certain behavior types as examples of costly employees. There are many types of *Red Ink Behavior* that translate to high costs in real dollars as well as stifled creativity and frustration in others. In this book, we highlight a few pure examples of those we frequently encounter in our coaching programs. Using the behavior types as models, we came to the realization that it was possible to set up a formula to measure the loss to the company across all levels of the employee's sphere of influence.

In Chapter One, we will describe some of these behaviors in more detail. For now we will tag the high maintenance employee as the *intimidator,* the *withholder,* the *controller,* the *stressor* or the *techno-bound executive* who can cause financial losses for the company. Those who are at the mercy of the

Red Ink Behavior become the victims and are also high maintenance executives who may cost everyone time and money.

The intimidator is the employee who stifles creativity in his staff, inhibits communication across functions, frightens his peers, blackmails and sabotages his boss. He can abuse subordinates and sabotage cross talk about problems or opportunities for *group thinking,* which he still does not believe beats *listening to himself talk.*

The withholder worker decreases the opportunity for productivity by **omitting essential information** which leaves whole groups in disarray for lack of crucial data. This do-it-yourselfer never builds a team, has no succession plan, is unable to collaborate and tends to discourage those who get in his way.

The controller/micro-manager is the employee who manhandles agendas, thwarts progress and causes resentment and fury around him. *He wants to be in charge of everything*— his boss, his peers, and, of course, every task that his subordinates are privileged to do for him. This micro-manager will always be burdened because he cannot prioritize—every task has the same charge!

The stressor executive is both a carrier and a raging recipient of stress. The stress carrier prevents peaceful decisions, detracts from action, shifts blame and direction and generally wastes time, his own and that of others. This type A behavioral pattern employee happily drops his or her stress on anyone in his sphere of influence. The sphere can be a big one, too, because they use flaming e-mails and lots of other indirect ways to produce tension for others. When he is tight with anxiety, his creativity and productivity diminishes. *The stressor scatters his impatience and frustration in his wake.*

The **techno-bound** puts most of his or her energy on the technical issues while the people problems are awarded back seat. This person is usually so technically smart that he collects "disposables" (people who are not as smart or competent as he is). If the boss happens to fall into that category, this grandiose employee simply does not attend his staff meetings! He may believe that he is brighter, more competent and more responsible than anyone else in the company, so he creates barriers around those whom he believes are not capable of producing.

The grandiose side of an employee, whether in a technical field or not, can take all the credit, give none away, and seems very unconscious about his territoriality and his abundance of "I" credits. Sometimes this is an introverted person who does not brag at all, but his technical grandiosity prevents handing out juicy assignments or distributing pivotal information.

Difficult employees take up time and energy from others. They also actually incite strong reactions in others. Some of those targeted victims take the reactions home. Other recipients quietly stir their ulcers at work over this self-centered employee who simply does not know how to read his impact on others.

For nearly twenty years our company, Growth & Leadership Center, has been trying to figure out how to save the conscientious employee who could not see the toll his behavior was taking on the company. We wanted to talk a manager or a human resource staff person into giving a difficult employee a chance at a remedial program. We knew that these stable employees were suffocating because they had not been working to their full potential.

Their managers recognized these employees, but they usually didn't know how to motivate them to change. The frustrated employees, then, who become under-appreciated, work in despair, not understanding why they are not promoted. The boss can't understand why he can't get this talented and conscientious employee to see the light.

The financial drain from an apparently outstanding employee is an insidious problem. It is not always easy to recognize the impact of someone who seems to have many extraordinary qualities. After interviewing their frustrated managers, we found that they did not always recognize the impact of these hidden actions which were subversive or non-collaborative. Sometimes the behavior was identified, but the high cost was still hard to assess. Only when we started asking about the time the boss loses trying to change or understand the employee, did we begin the intricate measuring program to calculate the high cost of that **Red Ink** employee.

Nobody likes to terminate an employee with skills and talents or history with customers. We knew we could help derailed employees get back on track. But we couldn't convince some companies that these executives might be worth the effort. Even when we would share glowing testimonials, some companies would balk, urging us to just stop talking about those tiresome employees who seemed unmanageable or unmotivated. Some were walking wounded, some were walking dead. Managers always felt inadequate and frustrated. Mind you, these employees were not usually terminated. They were left to fend for themselves, often without the responsibility they were used to, and always wondering why they were not compensated or promoted.

The employee remained tortured by his handicaps, not aware of his worst working style idiosyncrasies. This was also hard on the manager. The feeling of being an inadequate manager wears on the self esteem, so we were doubly eager to find a way to sell him on the idea that this employee may need some help.

It has been hard for companies to spend energy and resources when they could not measure the saving from an intervention. It is difficult to measure the costs or the results in morale, employee satisfaction, team camaraderie or in working group harmony. So the loss in these areas does not get the attention of those who can only relate to the cost of a new technical apparatus or a maintenance plan for a machine.

At the end of one of our successful team building programs, a client customer and good friend of mine who hired us, confessed to us that he also could have elected to spend the same amount of money on the very expensive piece of equipment which he needed. This is a moment frozen in time for our company. I was determined at that moment to try to find a way to convince him, in his terms, how to evaluate the cost of those fifteen employees whose teamsmanship was so weak, whose collaborative brain trust so dry, whose turnover rates were so bad, but I couldn't find a way to show him the high cost of some of those working styles at that time. Now I can.

Red Ink Behaviors are the working habits and idiosyncrasies of employees who drain their peers, subordinates and managers of useful time. The reaction to dysfunctional working habits or behaviors is the down time caused by unproductive or destructive behavior. The down time translation is our costimator—the way we calculate lost time from unproductive or draining work methods.

VI

We used a data base of 40 specific cases which were selected from the over 500 collected profiles from company and self-referrals who went through our leadership programs in the past five years. The 500 cases were scrutinized to determine the most prevalent problems we had encountered. All of these employees experienced our whole program, using five goals from the company and five for themselves, with interventions like video taping, theme groups, testing, observed staff meetings, and some one-on-one challenging and confrontive reality checks from our staff.

The objective was to deliver the ten goals back to the company and the employee. Therefore, to prevent career downturns in employees or their managers who could not see the cost of certain behaviors, and especially, to make our job easier, we designed a formula to measure the financial cost of these behaviors.

We measured time lost from the employee, his boss, peers and subordinates. We even included some human resources time loss. We calculated only the productive lost time, not the long term effects of lowered self esteem, empowerment issues for subordinates, or the esteem loss of the individual who feels untrusted or unappreciated

All too often executives don't wake up over ranking or rating or appraisals or trips to human resources. What sometimes finally gets their attention is the statement, from whatever source, that "NO ONE WANTS TO WORK WITH, FOR, OR OVER YOU!"

Even after the above statement, some executives still don't wake up. They rationalize and blame and turn their blind spots toward the problem, instead of being open to new data about their corporate behavior. This is why we are so excited to have one measurement tool to point out expensive and exhaustive behaviors earlier—before the point of no return. That point of no return happens when all trust is destroyed and the corporate scar tissue is so deep that the employee would be better off leaving the organization.

This measurement tool works in an athletic team or a church. It works in the three largest companies in Silicon Valley, for which we have the pleasure of consulting. It works in banks and in congress. It works on the technical bench and the legal bench.

With the hundreds of years of combined service in our company, from both sides of the corporate desk, we all believe this is a remarkable device. The notion of having a way to count difficult behavior is the most significant work of my personal career. I am happy to be able to present the following chapters. The data is yours to use and grow by. It is ours to sustain us in the work ahead. My friend who could measure the cost of a piece of machinery but not the cost of an evolved employee, will now have the hard facts from which to decide on a new piece of technology or a new piece of executive enhancement. It is yours to save you time, angst, confusion and financial loss.

This book does not require page by page reading. Jump in on the numerous cases where you have an interest. We sometimes repeat ourselves in the event that you do jump around. We think the idea bears repeating—**negative employees cost money.**

We think this may be a form of a breakthrough in the social psychology of working men and women. We hope you will use the formulas, work the numbers, and find the courage to show those numbers when an employee is not returning the company's investment in him. You owe it to the other employees who have learned how to change. You owe it to the company who gets drained by the costly behaviors. You owe it to an employee who wants to change and doesn't know how. We think it may save his professional life.

Warning: GLC programs are also offered to black ink high potential employees who have no major flaws and simply need leadership enhancement programs.

Jean Hollands, 1997

Chapter 1

What are Red Ink Behaviors?

Red Ink Behaviors are the working styles and habits which cost the company money. They are time losers for the employee, boss, peers and subordinates. The negative ramifications of poor judgment and ego-driven decisions are expensive. Our version of the cost is simply a financial one. We knew that top executives listen to bottom line numbers. We believed that translating negative behavior to dollars might get some attention. It did.

As we began to calculate the costs of problem behaviors of some of the employees we worked with, we were surprised by the results. Sifting through case after case, we discovered the cost impact of problem behaviors was larger than we had ever imagined. With all the ripples and side effects, it was not unusual to find fairly common negative behaviors with an annual cost of $50,000 to one million dollars, depending on the responsibility of the position and the hours lost by bosses, peers and subordinates.

The second result was the breakthrough. We began to see the process by which we could calculate the cost of errant behaviors. It was possible to take certain situations, run through a calculation, and approximate the annual cost of allowing the behavior to continue. We learned that just one loud outburst might cost the company something like $3000, but chronic temper outbursts could cost the company ten times that number every year!

The implications were enormous. Now, we reasoned, alternatives for resolving the situation could be evaluated in clear business terms. The ROI (Return on Investment), the pay-back period and the break-even point could be calculated. Some employees and their behaviors may ultimately be labeled not worth the return on investment. Others were worth the needed funds to correct or shift their behaviors in new directions.

Costly Employees Come in All Shapes and Sizes.

Across the ranks, from stock person to Chief Executive Officer, companies have employees who cost too much. They usually cost much more than their salaries or the salaries of many around them. This book will show you how to measure the extraordinary expense of the problem employee. With this information in hand, you are better able to consider your alternatives, weighing the cost of each against the ongoing cost of letting the problem continue.

Difficult employees can take up the boss's time, the security guard's time, the public relations officer's time, and they certainly take up time in the human relations department. How do you know if your company has a problem?

How Do We Know there is a Problem?

Problems repeated again and again in different company cultures and settings can be symptomatic of a problem employee, and, thus, Red Ink Behavior:

1. Everyone in a department is complaining about an individual in that department.
2. People in the company are doing everything they can to avoid working for a given manager, director or vice president.
3. People in that department show lower productivity than the rest of the company.
4. Deadlines are missed, budgets are overrun, quality is poor, and there are plenty of excuses.
5. Morale is poor. People show little enthusiasm, initiative, flexibility or self-responsibility.
6. Turnover and absenteeism are rampant in a group. Given a choice, people would rather not be there.
7. Performance reviews are chronically delivered late and poorly regarded by giver and receiver.

What Do The Problems Look Like?

GLC uses the following check-list to urge managers to take a look at some specific behaviors when they claim they have a difficult employee, but they can't seem to pinpoint a concrete habit or issue.

The careers of many brilliant, talented and high potential individuals have at times been derailed or slowed down because of performance shortcomings. Employees who demonstrate the following traits often sabotage their own potential and damage relationships with their team, managers, peers and subordinates.

Quick Checklist of Red Ink Behaviors
The Possible Consequences of Ambitious, Conscientious Leadership:

If you or a colleague experience significantly impaired performance due to any of the following symptoms, you may want to explore the consequences of these behaviors:

<u>Check Problem Areas:</u>

- □ Anger management: does not seem to channel hostility appropriately
- □ Arrogance about competency and interpersonal issues
- □ Attacks others or benign situations
- □ Authenticity: creates own spin and does not appear credible at times
- □ Awareness: does not perceive his/her impact on others
- □ Barriers: creates them unnecessarily and at will
- □ Collaboration: seems unable to cooperate or engender collaborative experiences
- □ Coaching: a do-it-yourselfer who cannot motivate or reinforce others
- □ Communication: fogs, monologues, inhibits productive dialogue
- □ Conflict Management: avoids or accelerates without resolution
- □ Consensus: ignores the possibility of its merit; uses only when lacking personal power
- □ Contradictory in minor and major discussions
- □ Controlling through micro-managing issues
- □ Credit: takes when not fully responsible

- Crisis Oriented: seems to create chaos
- Criticizes publicly and without regard to acceptance readiness
- Defensive: lobbies for own perception without fully hearing other points of view
- Dictatorial: not inclusive when in decision-making process
- Empathy: does not show appropriate care for others
- Evasive when data or action required
- Feedback: does not give or take feedback constructively
- Flexibility: does not easily adapt to changes in directions
- Friction: seems to attract or create conflict
- High maintenance: something always awry
- Humorless about self or decisions
- Impatient when perceiving incompetence
- Inflammatory: escalates difficult situations
- Inhibits creativity or power in situations and others
- Inspiration: inability to motivate others to action
- Listening: does not reflect back, listens selectively, more interested in being listened to
- Mentoring: seems unable to accept mentoring for self or provide mentoring to others
- Organizationally scattered
- Politically naive about resident and transient power
- Power: does not appear to empower others or use own power appropriately
- Priority: unable to maintain appropriate focus
- Procrastinates decisions and tasks
- Rapport: does not understand concept
- Reactionary: quick to act; impulsive in response
- Reading others: seems unable to accurately define his/her effect on others
- Reality check: often seems alone in his/her steadfast convictions; unwilling to seek feedback

- Reluctant to share knowledge, teach others, participate interactively
- Repair-ability: can't mend difficult situations
- Resistant to new ideas or difficult feedback
- Rigid: does not stay open to options
- Sarcastic: uses cryptic and cynical humor which puts others on guard and evokes distrust
- Strategy: does not maintain visionary understanding or big picture planning
- Stress: a stress manifestor and carrier!
- Team play: seems unable to create or stay involved as a team member
- Time-urgency predominates; unable to manage time
- Tolerance: seems intolerant under specific conditions
- Trust: unable to engender or experience trust with others
- Vulnerability: does not express fragility easily
- Uncooperative: does not manage up, down or with peers
- Unempowered: little responsibility for directing own career
- Withholds information

Why Do These Problems Happen in Otherwise Talented Employees?

We want to show examples of behaviors which become habits even with the best of intentions. These behaviors are so obvious to others while they are blind spots to the individual.

Aggressive. Arrogant. Controlling. Micro-managing. These are some of the characteristics which label certain employees who eventually become problems for a company. But how did a brilliant executive with a first class education and will to help others eventually become a candidate for derailment? These employees adopt and sustain behaviors because they were initially reinforced for the behavior. That very behavior is now derailing them, and tripping up their colleagues, and their own chances for success.

The following are dramatic examples, offered from a composite of some of the executives we all encounter:

Edgar

Edgar, MIS Director in a large materials company, was a long-term employee. After years of frustration, Edgar was evaluated by his seven peers and fourteen direct reports. You will note that fourteen reports is extraordinary. This is just one symptom of Edgar's controlling management style. He could not let go of any of his spans of interest, and, of course, he believed he needed jurisdiction over a large sphere of the company. He was very difficult to dislodge because of his arrogant style.

Edgar was one of the smartest boys in the school. In the first grade, he remembers the teacher asking him to erase the blackboards (no whiteboards then.) She always asked him to help. He liked this, and he did not notice the other kids' jealousy. In fact, for the next five or six years, the smart kids, the smart-alec kids and the teacher's pets were always elected to class officers and monitors and all of the fun activities of growing up.

In junior high, things tightened up a bit. The teacher was still praising and urging his creativity, but the other kids were not as enthused. Sometimes they looked disgusted with Edgar, but he was too busy feeling righteous to note his social failures with the class. When he ridiculed the eighth grade science teacher, though, kids applauded him. That was the first time he had experienced special attention in a very long time.

You know the rest of Edgar's story. He went on to be Teaching Assistant in college, always being first in the class and always asking intelligent and provocative questions in labs. Instructors enjoyed his quick mind and probing questions.

Edgar took the probing questions to his first job, and he was recognized and promoted accordingly. People grew a little wary of him, but no one questioned his mind or his intentions to get the right answers! Edgar's peers found his arrogant style frustrating. The more courageous colleagues took him on, and because it was hard to win, they also found ways to sabotage his work, trying to make Edgar look bad.

The conflict averse peers simply looked the other way. They spent extra hours going around Edgar, obtaining information from other sources in circuitous and expensive ways. They often forgot Edgar's requests, which ultimately cost Edgar working time as well. The high maintenance costs of keeping Edgar around began to take their toll. This was not a team environment. Yet no one seemed able or willing to stand up to Edgar.

Until...they got tired of him. Until...the boss got disgusted with the belittling way he started the questions. Until...he seemed to point out errors just to draw attention to himself.

Until...Edgar became a disrupting influence in every meeting in which he participated.

Why Are They Allowed to Stick Around?

An employee like Edgar is the indispensible specialist in an area. Nobody understands his technology like Edgar. Of course, he has prepared himself to be indispensable, the only man with the key to the safe. However, people like Edgar do eventually get fired, downgraded, demoted, dethroned. They deliver one comment too many, they infuriate the boss or the visiting customer, and they now become a detriment. Until that moment, though, they stick around because they serve a valuable purpose. They do work that no one else can or wants to do. These difficult employees protect their boss in certain areas, they work long hours, they don't complain about business trips, or they simply come up with the right answer at the right time.

They stick around because the company finds them hard to retrain or replace. They simply can't give up the show-off-or-die belief system. They are not affected by the ordinary warning procedures. Feedback from others seems invalid because people like Edgar believe they are the only judge of their conduct, or in fact, of anyone else's conduct. This self-centeredness prevents employees from weighing their actual impact on others.

These employees often bully their bosses or any decision-maker who could question their antics. They bully by feeding in the right materials at the right time to make the department look good. The boss thinks he will have to work harder himself if the likes of an Edgar stops selling or inventing or calculating for a single day. Edgar always gets the last word in public debates because his logical mind pulls out the appropriate response, but he ignores the impact on the embarrassed opponent.

Edgar will hit below the belt if he has to. He then becomes an intimidating debater, especially to the person who goes pre-verbal in the face of a sarcastic blast. The victim is reduced to the equivalent of a two-year old who simply does not have the words to retort to Edgar. Edgar wins.

Another reason they stay around is that they usually find a support person with whom to collude. This person needs Edgar's brain, or perhaps he is another sarcastic Edgar who is never afraid in a debate. The two or three of them stick together so that all of them can stay sticking around.

What's An Intervention?

An intervention is any action taken to attempt to inform or change Edgar. These suggestions come in many forms: appraisals (we are usually sent two inches worth of appraisals for the most problem-plagued employees.) Other actions include trips to Human Resources, memos, meetings with his boss, his boss's boss and with anyone who has the courage to try to get through to difficult Edgar.

An intervention may be a class, a book, a confrontive meeting, any opportunity for the employee to understand his impact on the organization. Our company is an intervention. Unfortunately, sometimes our program is the court of last resort. We are looking for an earlier detection process so employees and companies don't have to suffer as long.

What Happens When You Try an Intervention?

They sometimes bomb. Edgar has all the answers. He does not believe the feedback. He interrogates the messenger with:

Can you give me a precise example of that behavior?
Who made that statement and when?
Do you know every fact surrounding this situation?
Have you derived the proper conclusion based on the right context?

If Edgar does not interrogate, he defensively reacts with such disruption that you are soon sorry you started anything. He may then pout, growl or hide for days or weeks at a time. This logical human being becomes very illogical when confronted.

What Does This Employee Cost the Organization?

The measurable cost is down time for everyone affected by him; the secretary, his peers, his subordinates, his boss. What do they do? They fume, they become humiliated, they pout or cry or choose to avoid the behavior and the surrounding projects. Or they complain to others about him. These frustrating conversations take time and energy. They rob the company of productive or creative work.

Sometimes fellow workers plot to get Edgar! This takes a lot of work. The slippery Edgar is not easy to trip up, and then, if you do catch him, you must suffer the consequences of his belligerent defenses. So the company pays for his down time. The company also pays for the down time of colleagues who exchange productivity for retribution in order to pay Edgar back for his abuse.

Edgar can also cost customers and big contracts. He causes chronically bad relationships with customers. This requires more favors to be done for those abused by Edgar. Eventually all of the dysfunctional habits of controlling, finger-pointing and temper tantrums show up in customer relations. Goodwill between departments or customers is measured by the extent of Edgar's infractions. All the while he maintains his denial that he is the cause of so much tension, confusion or low morale.

Definitions for the following Costimators:

Pay back (months): The return on training investment.

Salary All salaries should include the benefits package which usually amounts to 30% of base pay. Also include bonuses and commissions.

Revenue Responsibilities: This should approximate the total gross sales or production costs which the candidate affects by his actions.

Loss in Revenues: The approximate percentage of his influence on the preceeding number.

GLC program cost: A number which any organization may charge for development work for this employee.

Opportunity cost to company: While the employee is spending time off the job to take a program, what percent is lost to the company above his actual hours away? This is the cost of loss of leadership, inspiration or organization which the employee embodies while he is there. This percentage of time away is added to program duration hours in the formula to account for total program cost.

Sunk cost: The amount spent in one year or in the <u>duration</u> noted on this employee.

Burn rate: The monthly cost of maintaining this employee with current problems.

Replacement costs: The amount to acquire a new employee in that position.

Costimator for Edgar

GLC Red Ink Behavior - Costimator Analysis

Please supply the following information: ID: 46

* Include all benefits in salaries (e.g., stocks, bonuses, insurances, etc...)

Last:		First: Edgar	Company CCC
Title:	MIS Dir		
Problem Description:	Arrogant - Intimidator		

Salary ($K/yr)*:	350	Severance package ($K):	350
DEP's lost hours/week:	1	Search hiring ($K):	100
Problem duration (Mo):	12	Training ($K):	25
Direct Cost:	**$8,750**	**Replacement Cost:**	**$475,000**

Manager's sal ($K/yr)*:	550	HR person's sal ($K/yr)*:	100
Manager's lost hrs/wk:	2	HR person's lost hrs/wk:	2
Dur.of intervention (Mo):	3	Other persons ($K/wk):	0
Intervention Cost:		**$8,125**	

Number of peers:	7	Number of subordinates:	14
Peers' salary ($K/yr)*:	350	Subordinates' salary ($K/yr)*:	210
Peers' lost hrs/wk:	3	Subordinates' lost hrs/wk:	4
Impact Cost (People):		**$477,750**	

Revenues responsibilities ($K)	100	GLC program cost ($K):	12
Loss on revenues (%):	3	GLC program duration (hrs):	16
		Opportunity cost to company (%):	30
Impact Cost (Revenues):	**$3,000**	**GLC Program Total Cost:**	**$15,792**

Sunk Cost ($):	**$497,625**	**Replacement Cost:**	**$475,000**
Burn Rate ($/Mo)	**$43,500**	**Payback (Mo):**	**0.4**

What's Another Problem Employee? The Stressor

The typical Silicon Valley overworked employee is another example of problem behaviors which can be expensive. We'll call this employee the Stressor. These employees are usually both the patient and the carrier. They believe they have the world on their shoulders.

The high-stress employees make good workers for awhile. They never say no, work all hours, and seem to be super-stars, perhaps...until they die. Until they die of heart attacks or immune system diseases. Or until they get chronically ill. Because they are so good and get so much done, they are often rewarded for lack of balance in their lives, especially if it is weighted toward the company. Eventually they go into paralytic burn-out.

Susan

They also cause stress in others. They interrupt, make scenes, rush others and generally upset everyone in their wake. Susan is a good example. When she, a middle manager, has to have a report done, she moves the world to get it done. Papers fly, people fly, and tempers fly. Her work is the most important task for everyone in the office and she is hysterically at the mercy of what she perceives to be lack of time.

Let's discuss Susan, who is the marketing manager in a progressive and successful computer company. Susan earns about $150,000 a year and has six subordinates who remain frustrated, often get themselves sick, or they stay in an everlasting state of unrest. Her four peers are often dis- gruntled and hurried themselves because their overlapping responsibilities are always usurped by Susan's

15

latest crisis. They all spend extra hours problem-solving for Susan or rearranging their own tasks because Susan is late with her part of the work. Susan, of course, never has enough time to even hear the complaints from her peers or subordinates.

Stressed employees usually have the *not enough* syndrome; not enough time, resources, love, money or appreciation. They complain a lot, but usually while on the run. People catch the disease from Susan, like a cold, because not getting enough is such a contagious possibility. There are so many ways to be measured in our adult life, so that empty emotional bank accounts are pervasive. If Susan awakens in you your own *not enough* response, you, too, can start running to the finance office or engineering, to hurry the procedure. If you are immune, maybe you received the lifetime shot against stress. If so, you are lucky. Most of us are too busy to get the shot. Of course, the vaccination is attitude. This is much harder to obtain than your basic flu shot.

Why Do These Behaviors Happen?

Susan is an employee powered by adrenaline which courses through her body and motivates her to meet deadlines and do super-human tasks. The college crammers were addicted to the rush of the last minute to study for exams. They cannot study without a tight deadline. You find these fire-fighters in every department. They are crisis-junkies and making a crisis is quite easy if you do not prioritize or plan for your activities. These folks invite stress in everyone else to get things done at the last frantic moment. On the other hand, some people, being stressors themselves, will love the anxious crisis-producing behavior.

There will be others, though, who do not welcome flash fires or reactionary behaviors. They will be disturbed, can shut down and rebel in a quieter way. They will reluctantly and passive-aggressively produce imperfect data for the compulsive Susan. Those employees who do plan ahead feel no compunction about bad work when procrastinating conditions demand it. Susan, of course, who will jump through hoops for last-minute assignments, cannot understand this insubordination at any level.

In our study of stressed employees we collaborated with the Myer Friedman Institute. Their ground-breaking discovery of Type A behaviors in heart attack candidates matches our conclusions about many of those referred to us for executive coaching.

Jeff Lugerner, a consultant for both the Friedman Institute and GLC, sees these clients regularly. Here is what we all conclude it is like to work with Type A behavior employees:

> Everything is a crisis
> Everything is important
> Everything is now
> There is always a problem
> Someone is always at fault

The Friedman Institute goes on to identify four common responses to the normal surprises of the work world in a Type A employee:

> Aggravation
> Irritation
> Anger
> Impatience

The stressed person often contradicts, lectures, sounds inflexible, doesn't seem to listen and talks fast, and, the most prominent symptom of all, interrupts.

Type A's demonstrate a free-floating hostility which presents as tense, critical, tenacious, demanding and fault-finding which usually puts off peers and workers who must interact with this difficult employee.

Why Are They Allowed to Stick Around?

For long periods of time, the stressed employee can get away with being the hero. This self-imposed hero gets so much work done. He or she often blames the cycles of work, faulty technology or ends of the quarter for his own procrastination.

While they are in their productive mood, these Susans are priceless. In one of our costimator cases which we presented to a Human Resource executive, we suggested that the company send Susan for a week's stay in Hawaii. The HR executive was appalled that we suggested a stressor would receive a week's stay anywhere.

"Our company would not even give her a weekend," she reported about her very successful but conservative company.

The manager neglected to add that her company would reward the Susans of the world with stock bonuses and large profit-sharing benefits. Susan might also be compensated with a new rating and thus, new salary. The mixed messages stressed employees receive sometimes reinforces the problem behavior.

What Happens When You Try an Intervention?

Sometimes you just feel silly. Susan has produced beyond the norm, and you are complaining? She makes you feel a little foolish when she brings out her list of accomplishments or she recites her litany of lost birthdays, holidays and the many hours she works. The interventionist must stick to his guns with, "Susan, I know you have really sacrificed for the company, but prioritization and good planning might have prevented the sacrifices."

Stressors can also reply with depression. "Well, if I'm not appreciated after all I've been through, I may as well give up." She will do all or nothing thinking. She is usually a rigid, compulsive person who does not know how to balance her life. She will rush to the other end of the extreme with depression and apathy.

If her adrenaline can't be stimulated, as a result of rushing, over-activity or self-imposed judgments, she will suffer. She will feel boredom with the quietude and believe that something is wrong. She can't get motivated unless there is a crisis. The fear of the underlying depression which can accompany low activity will motivate Susan to stay in high activity.

What Does a Stressor Cost the Organization?

Thousands and thousands of dollars! Her own work eventually suffers. She is known to go home with a migraine the night before the trade show. Of course, she has half of the slides and models in her car or her own head, so she brings the migrained head to the show, moaning and groaning over her fragile life, while guilt falls all around. The trade show suffers, work is incomplete and not quality driven. Pieces are missing and the company looks bad.

Susan's boss loses sleep over the work not finished, and gives a poor key-note address at the conference. He doesn't feel he can complain when poor old Susan came to the trade show when she was feeling so bad. So the boss feels frustrated, with no target for the angst, and, thus, inappropriately picks on other employees.

Susan's staff members always manage to need to take off sick or personal time after big deadlines. Susan does too. Since these are not planned absences, the whole department suffers from those who are at home and not interlocking with other work in the department.

The cost to the human resource department is abundant and also frustrating. The disease is so insidious because Susan appears to be a loyal and good worker. When she is on, she is great. The cost of erratic behavior is not only the way she does things that causes wide-spread despair and lack of trust, but it is not always easily spotted.

Susan's peers and her boss suffer from her stressed Type A style. They dread her approach to their offices and they often do the work themselves, robbing themselves of their creative time, rather than have Susan make one of her big deals out of it.

Susan's Costimator

GLC Red Ink Behavior   -   Costimator Analysis

Please supply the following information:	ID:	47

* Include all benefits in salaries (e.g., stocks, bonuses, insurances, etc...)

Last:		First:	Susan	Company	SRW
Title:	Mktg Mgr				
Problem Description:	Stressor				

Salary ($K/yr)*:	150	Severance package ($K):	150
DEP's lost hours/week:	3	Search hiring ($K):	50
Problem duration (Mo):	12	Training ($K):	12
Direct Cost:	**$11,250**	**Replacement Cost:**	**$212,000**

Manager's sal ($K/yr)*:	350	HR person's sal ($K/yr)*:	60
Manager's lost hrs/wk:	3	HR person's lost hrs/wk:	3
Dur.of intervention (Mo):	3	Other persons ($K/wk):	0
Intervention Cost:		**$7,688**	

Number of peers:	4	Number of subordinates:	6
Peers' salary ($K/yr)*:	150	Subordinates' salary ($K/yr)*:	80
Peers' lost hrs/wk:	2	Subordinates' lost hrs/wk:	4
Impact Cost (People):		**$78,000**	

Revenues responsibilities ($K)	200	GLC program cost ($K):	12
Loss on revenues (%):	2	GLC program duration (hrs):	20
		Opportunity cost to company (%):	30
Impact Cost (Revenues):	**$4,000**	**GLC Program Total Cost:**	**$14,031**

Sunk Cost ($):	**$100,938**	**Replacement Cost:**	**$212,000**
Burn Rate ($/Mo)	**$10,333**	**Payback (Mo):**	**1.4**

What's Another Costly Problem?
The Micro-manager:

Charlie

Charlie is an Engineering Director for a computer networking corporation. With five peers directly affected by his over-management and seven managers who work for Charlie, the company is losing resources based on Charlie's inappropriate priorities.

The micro-manager costs his company losses in creativity, spontaneity and initiative. The paradox about this controlling micro-manager is that he believes he is so responsible, so careful, so diligent, that he has no idea of the expense he is to his organization.

The micro-manager loses reflection and strategic thinking time because he continues to check and recheck until there is no available time for big picture thinking. His conceptual planning time is reduced to walking out to the parking lot.

Charles, the controlling manager, will drive his employees crazy. Ultimately no one wants to work for him because he thwarts any autonomy or individuality in his subordinates. They spend no time in creative thinking because they are so busy following Charles' rules. His employees become wary of any change, fearing the change will create more procedural minutia for them. They avoid anything which will cause them more work, thus, ignoring an opportunity for productive changes which could be more efficient. The combination of a Charles and a rebel subordinate is disastrous. The rebel will spend countless hours trying to thwart Charles' guidelines. He won't follow the rules and Charles can create more rebels with

his controlling ways. Charles does not tell his employees
WHY. He tells them **HOW.**

When a creative employee feels he can't plan his own time or
work his own agenda, he becomes apathetic or rebellious,
depending on his own reactionary style. In either case,
Charles' subordinates waste time trying to get out of Charles'
laborious work. His peers waste time going around Charles
for the same reason as his subordinates. Everything is a chore
and everything must be done Charles' way. Peers do not
invite him to extra planning meetings, which in the long run
causes more work for everyone, with Charles' quality assurance maneuvers eventually upsetting the strategic planning.

How Do These Behaviors Happen?

Charlie, the micro-manager, usually has some internal fears
that unless he does something perfectly, it is not good enough.
He does not buy the 80-20% rule, and lives by the judge
inside, who says, "If you can't do it right the first time, don't
do it." Those internal judges come from his first boss, his
sixth grade school teacher, and often from parents who
instilled the quality of one's work value. Only Charlie carries
the message too far. He can't tell the difference between
important work and less important work. He applies the same
standard of his quality work ethic for every task.

The compulsivity to check is a burdensome handicap.
Charlie can't relax. He has to control everything and everyone
he can get his hands on. No job is good enough, finished
enough, or ready enough. He stalls his colleagues who may
just want the status of the job, not the complete report.
Charlie, the perfectionist, is also the procrastinator. He tries
so hard to get everything in order before he makes a call that

it takes longer than necessary. His assignments to his people, then, are expensively late. He wants to include all the details and do all the thinking for them. They also wait for details, (which live in his head alone), so they become inactive and non-responsive to the dilemmas which only Charlie manages.

Why Are These People Allowed to Stick Around?

Employees like Charles appear to be well organized, a trait we all crave from others. We admire those who seem to have everything under control, particularly if their work overlaps some of our own responsibilities. Everyone believes his own organizational skills are flawed, so, of course, we desire this revered skill in our colleagues. It takes a long, expensive toll to discover that he is not as organized as he appears. He spends a lot of time talking about what should or could be done, with less time on the actual implementation phase. He loves to collect data and get ready.

We keep these employees because they are usually not overtly rebellious. They are, however, success impostors. They show an enthusiasm for quality. They talk about quality a lot. They simply cannot live up to their own standards. Unfortunately, we don't find this out early enough. When we do try to give evaluations, Charles is so controlling that he can send the evaluator off on the wrong tangent.

Some of the controller's subordinates do not complain because they are craving the judgment and measurement of a militant boss. These masochistic individuals feel comfortable with micro-management. Their parents or former athletic coaches treated them with a judgment/discipline cycle and they still believe they need this rigid structure to perform.

The problem is that some micro-managers don't give the rewards for the same things they measure. Charlie adds to his problems because he believes his people never do enough, and surely they don't do things according to his instructions. If he could explain **WHY** a task needs to be performed, he might get some cooperation and good work back. Instead, communication is often muffled with too much detail. Rework becomes the order of the day for his people.

What Happens When You Try an Intervention?

When a problem is exposed, Charlie will report on the incompetencies of his employees or even his peers. He is not shy about his boss' failures either. No one, not even his boss, follows directions well enough for Charles. So when Charles is confronted about his micro-management or lack of delegation, he falls into reporting on the shortcomings of others: The "everybody else is not OK" syndrome.

When Charles receives further warnings or feedback, he resorts to his crisis backup behavior and becomes dramatically more compulsive and controlling. This character does not usually have much of a sense of humor. In his conflict mode, Charles is all business - detailed, rigid and punctilious. He loses the big picture and the company loses money.

What Does This Behavior Cost the Organization?

Charlie cannot do succession planning because he is so consumed with doing everything right. He knows that there is no one alive who can do his job as well as he can. So he does no coaching, assuming no one can learn.

He puts off anything his boss contributes because he judges that the boss has not taken every detail into consideration. The boss loses productive time from him because Charlie re-thinks all decisions. The boss loses collaboration time with his peer level because Charlie cannot give him incremental goals or status reports unless everything is in Charlie's order. Charlie micro-manages his boss, colleagues and subordinates. His colleagues resent doing reports in his form. "I'm not going to make this request in Prince Charles's form," bellows his peer, the marketing manager.

Charlie's peers and subordinates lose productive time because they are stumped over a trivial detail Charlie seems to require. Peers often cut Charlie out of the collaborative loop, and meetings when they can, because they see him as a block to creativity and productivity. In this process they may miss important data which Charlie squirrels away, fearful of giving away too much information to the perilous peer strata. Charlie invites confusion, frustration and often unconsciously sabo-tages real opportunities for collaborative efforts. His col-leagues can't live with him or without him. In each case, the company pays...

Costimator for Charles

GLC Red Ink Behavior　-　Costimator Analysis

Please supply the following information:　　　　　　　ID: | 48

* Include all benefits in salaries (e.g., stocks, bonuses, insurances, etc...)

Last:		First:	Charlie	Company	CCC Co
Title:	Eng Dr				
Problem Description:	Micro Mgr				

Salary ($K/yr)*:	270	Severance package ($K):	270
DEP's lost hours/week:	0	Search hiring ($K):	100
Problem duration (Mo):	12	Training ($K):	15
Direct Cost:	**$0**	**Replacement Cost:**	**$385,000**

Manager's sal ($K/yr)*:	400	HR person's sal ($K/yr)*:	80
Manager's lost hrs/wk:	0	HR person's lost hrs/wk:	0
Dur.of intervention (Mo):	3	Other persons ($K/wk):	0
Intervention Cost:		**$0**	

Number of peers:	5	Number of subordinates:	7
Peers' salary ($K/yr)*:	270	Subordinates' salary ($K/yr)*:	150
Peers' lost hrs/wk:	2	Subordinates' lost hrs/wk:	4
Impact Cost (People):		**$172,500**	

Revenues responsibilities ($K)	500	GLC program cost ($K):	15
Loss on revenues (%):	2	GLC program duration (hrs):	30
		Opportunity cost to company (%):	30
Impact Cost (Revenues):	**$10,000**	**GLC Program Total Cost:**	**$20,484**

Sunk Cost ($):	**$182,500**	**Replacement Cost:**	**$385,000**
Burn Rate ($/Mo)	**$15,208**	**Payback (Mo):**	**1.3**

What to Do With a Micro-Manager

1. Name the problem. Tell your micro-manager exactly what you see. You will have to be scrupulous and meticulous with the feedback in order to get his attention. Name the exact behavior which frustrated or de-motivated others. Calculate the overall cost of lost time in the others and in extra work which only the micro-manager was interested in having.

2. Create consequences and rewards. Reinforce the slightest change in behavior. When his list is shorter than usual, the level of detail is not so thorough, when the report is a little less rigid, compliment him. Suggest that you know it is hard to give up the last 20% precision, but remind him that you are glad he did only the important part of the project.

3. Offer consequences for continued waste of company time and resources. Use reviews, promotion possibilities and most of all, use diminishment of responsibilities as wake-up calls. The controlling micro-manager loves new challenges. He would really like all new technical tasks assigned to him. When he begins to see that challenging and technical opportunities may be withdrawn from him, he may begin to get the message. "Charles, I didn't give you this job, because I knew you would make it too burdensome for others, and you would take too long to complete it. I know you would have liked to do it, but it would have been too expensive to use you on this project."

4. Keep reminding your micro-manager that you are not encouraging sloppy work. You are wanting him or her to prioritize his time and resources and apply energy where it offers the most company rewards, not because she or he enjoys the counting of the beans! When your micro-person catches

himself with prioritizing and checks with you on what he should not be doing, you probably have a much better manager in the making. Assign tasks that do call for accuracy in which he or she can feel the rewards of a meticulous approach. Then explain the tasks that call for a more pragmatic approach.

<u>Warning:</u> <u>GLC programs are also offered to black ink high potential employees who have no major flaws and simply need leadership enhancement programs.</u>

Chapter Two

How the Costimator Came About

The costimator is the happy result of frustration and challenge. GLC has worked with dozens of major Silicon Valley companies at all levels of management. Over the years we have seen a recurring problem incredibly costly to business, one that drives all to distraction and can literally cripple major parts of a corporation. And yet, it rarely comes to the attention of the decision-maker as a priority business issue.

The decision-makers naturally focus on the bottom line. They spend their time and energy on product and marketing issues for which measurable results can be shown in revenues, expenses, and profits. The focus is rarely on the high impact yet difficult to measure money gobblers called **people dynamics.** Where people skills are lacking, the side effects may be devastating. The negative impact is to stifle and limit creative initiative and a sense of taking real responsibility and owner-

ship for results. When the offender is a key manager, it affects
the performance of that person, his or her manager, peers, and
subordinates. It can easily affect the revenue production.

For years, GLC has worked with business after business to
identify, prevent, and cure problematic people behaviors. We
are in the business of changing habits and beliefs that serve
poorly in the business arena.

Often the need for a remedy is clear enough. What is missing
is the cost justification and imperative to take immediate
corrective action. After all, the company has lived with the
problem until now and there are always other matters that
appear more tangible in terms of return on investment.

GLC believes that the elusive cost determination too often
causes a ready excuse for procrastination, however debilitating,
to the effectiveness of the business unit. If the true return on
investment were ever understood, we reasoned, a company
would be able to treat this much like a decision to buy a new
piece of equipment or to launch a marketing campaign.

Early inquiries confirmed our suspicion that the problem is just
as frustrating for the line executive and the HR manager. Each
is in the position of experiencing and/or observing the effects
of the behavior without being able to quantify the dollar impact
of resolving the problems. Left unclear, the problems are left
to fester and worsen while other issues (perhaps far less
important) receive prompt attention.

The Costimator was borne out of this perplexing need. GLC
undertook a very deliberate study of dozens of its case histories
to identify and analyze the types of cost and the methodology
of quantifying the dollar impact of resolution versus letting the
behavior continue.

Technical Aspects of the Costimator

The Costimator is an instrument developed to quantify the dollar impact of an employee's negative behavior on the company, as a function of a set of data describing the situation. The goal is to express this monetary cost in a unit that describes the company losses *per unit of time* if the behavior remains un-addressed, the "burn rate per week," for example. One can also derive other measures, such as a total cost per year to be compared with the employee's salary. Furthermore, if an intervention is envisioned and if its cost is known, several economic indexes can be easily calculated, such as the return on investment rate and the pay-back time.

Simple calculations easily show that these figures are "somewhere" in the thousands of dollars, but nobody has ever approached the question scientifically and reached a "floor" estimate. Our study has shown that the real figures are even more mind boggling, amounting to the tens and sometimes the hundreds of thousands of dollars. These findings lead us to conclude that the best way to serve our clients is to provide them with a simple systematic tool to estimate these wastes and make timely decisions to cut their losses.

Concepts and History

We identified five major areas of cost: direct costs, sphere of influence costs, impact on revenues, intervention costs, and, eventually, replacement cost.

It was clear that the end-result, the cost of the behavior in dollars per week, should be a function of variables such as yearly salary, number of peers, number of subordinates, etc... The early model, while covering a wide variety of situations, quickly appeared over-encompassing and difficult to test. We simplified it in several ways.

First we elected to match the precision of the calculations with that of the data. This is to say that, since our data is typically an "approximation", we grouped as a single variable (the number of hours lost per week) the various components of the impact of the employee's behavior on his peers and subordinates. We also assumed that only one manager and one HR person are involved in the situation.

Then, we made the assumption that there are two distinct sets of values: the behavioral parameters and the situational variables.

1. Behavioral Parameters

We assumed that these values are characteristic of the behavior and remain constant across situations. We have selected six measures as characteristic of each behavior:

Time lost by the employee (TE, in hours per week)

Time employee loses each week as a consequence of problem behavior. It includes unproductive time spent demonstrating the behavior as well as time to recover from it that could be used more productively for the company.

Time lost by his/her manager (TM, in hours per week)

Time lost by employee's manager to deal with the behavior and consequences. Includes extraneous one-on-one meeting, memo writing, consulting with others, and aggravation.

Time lost by HR person involved (TH, in hours per week)

Downtime lost by HR person involved in resolution of the problem behavior. Includes listening to complaints, attempting to mediate a conflict, and all other activities that the HR person will perform above and beyond his or her regular obligations.

Time lost by the peers of the employee (TP, in hours per week)

Time lost by the employee's peers as a consequence of the behavior. This includes time wasted in waiting for information or product, mediating, complaining, and aggravation.

Time lost by employees subordinates(TS, in hours per week)

Time lost by the employee's subordinates as a consequence of problem behavior. Includes loss of productivity, poor morale, lack of motivation, fear, stifled creativity, resentment and/or passive resistance, etc...

Percentage lost of employee's company revenues (PC)

Percentage of company revenues that the employee is in charge of that is lost as a consequence of behavior. Includes lost contracts, lost clients, or opportunities. This value is estimated in percentage form to cancel out the impact of the size of the company on the size of the revenues.

2. Situational Parameters

These values are assumed to be situation specific and independent of the behavior. They are generally "well known" and easy to collect. We have selected the following measures as descriptive of the situation (All salaries include an estimate of the benefits such as medical insurance, profit sharing, stock options, bonuses, etc....):

Employee's salary

Manager's salary

HR salary

Number of peers

Peer's salary

Number of subordinates

Subordinate's salary

Leaving for the second phase (Use of the Formula) the specification of the situational unknowns, we have, in a first phase, validated the parameters.

Validation Approach
The Problem

It is not as easy to define and measure a negative behavior and its consequences as it is to measure the weight or height of an employee. Consequently, the conceptualization of the impact cost of such behaviors has typically remained vague and therefore inaccurate. The usual scientific approach to developing a formula reflecting the relation between behavior and dollar impact is impeded by our lack of understanding of such a relation. To resolve this problem, we have chosen to use a tool known as the Delphi method.

The Delphi Method Approach

In the Delphi method, we ask a group of experts to quantitatively estimate a non-measurable variable, such as the time per week wasted on the job by an employee as a consequence of a certain pattern of behavior. There are two assumptions behind such an approach: (1) once specified, the behavior pattern is easily recognizable, presents the same features across individuals, and can be described by a few parameters with approximately the same values across situations; and (2) the experts in the group are familiar with the behaviors and have lived through their consequences.

The experts are polled independently and anonymously to avoid influencing each other. Each is presented with five vignettes describing five situations and a set of six quantitative questions about each situation. These six questions address the six variables that we have selected as descriptive of each situation. The responses are averaged to obtain a **consensus value for each parameter**.

If the standard deviation of a parameter appears high, thus showing a lack of consensus, a second round is performed with another vignette, focusing on this parameter. This protocol yielded five sets of six variables which are the five formulas of the Costimator.

We developed a set of five vignettes based on a sorting of the cases drawn from our company files. This yielded five major problem behaviors. From this study, we derived a cost formula for each, and we believe these five formulas will cover most cases one would encounter in the daily life of a corporation.

The Results of the Study

We enrolled eight experts from leading Silicon Valley companies to review the five scenarios and estimate the five sets of six variables.

These results confirm the difficulty of evaluating these parameters and dictate a conservative approach in retaining final values. We chose to retain, for each of the 30 values, the mean minus one standard deviation to increase the chances of having a "floor" estimate. In the case of strong outliers, the means and standard deviations have been recalculated after replacing the outliers with their corresponding extreme, the minimum or the maximum. For reasons of time, this approach was chosen over the alternative (re-polling the group of experts on each question).

This technique yielded the following sets of values:

	Employee's Time	Manager's Time	HR's Time	Peers' Time	Subordinates' Time	Impact on Revenues
Intimidator	3.5	1.0	1.5	1.5	4.5	6.5%
Stressed	12.5	1.5	3.5	2.5	7.0	3.5%
Micro-Mgr	11.5	0.5	1.0	1.5	7.0	3.0%
Victim	5.0	2.0	3.5	1.5	2.5	2.5%
Tech-(Wo)man	5.0	0.5	1.0	1.0	3.5	6.0%

Use of the Formula

Once the five formulas are established and the parameters estimated, the next step consists of applying it to a real situation which will supply the situational unknowns to complete the calculation of the formula.

Identify a Potential Target (Company/Executive)Not all situations can be evaluated with this tool. Some behaviors can be too extreme or too exceptional and would not be appropriately described by the Costimator formula. More specifically, if a behavior is not at least approximately described by one of the five vignettes, it would not be wise to attempt to use the Costimator formula to draw a conslusion about the cost of this behavior. Instead, use *your own* specific data collected for hours lost in each category.

Collect the Specific Information

Once the target is identified and matched with one of the five formulas described above, the manager or the HR person in charge of the issue is consulted to obtain the values of the situational variables.

The Results of the Study

We enrolled eight experts from leading Silicon Valley companies to review the five scenarios and estimate the five sets of six variables. The following tables show the results for each of the five cases. It indicates the mean, standard deviation and range of each of the six variables. These six vriables were defined above as behavioral parameters.

In all tables, the five columns on the left represent expenditure of time in hours per week, and the column on the far right represents the percent of the total company revenues the employee is responsible for. The bold print represents the outliers or single extreme answers to a specific question.

The following five tables show the values for the five sample cases we used.

Case #1: The Intimidator

Hrs/Week	Employee's Time	Manager's Time	HR's Time	Peers' Time	Subs' Time	Impact on Revenues
Expert #1	6.00	0	15	8	8	10
Expert #2	5.00	4	6	3	3	**40**
Expert #3	1.50	3	4	6	8	15
Expert #4	6.00	3	1	2	10	7
Expert #5	**20.00**	2	2	2	10	5
Expert #6	10.00	2	10	5	10	10
Expert #7	8.00	4	4	2	4	10
Expert #8						
Average	8.07	2.57	6.00	4.00	7.57	13.86
SD	5.88	1.40	4.93	2.38	2.94	11.94
Minimum	1.50	0.00	1.00	2.00	3.00	5.00
Maximum	20.00	4.00	10.00	6.00	10.00	40.00

Case #2: The Stressed Executive

Hrs/Week	Employee's Time	Manager's Time	HR's Time	Peers' Time	Subs' Time	Impact on Revenues
Expert #1	12.00	1	3	3	6	
Expert #2	15.00	5	8	3	8	5
Expert #3	20.00	8	8	10	12	30
Expert #4	20.00	4	4	3	8	2
Expert #5	20.00	2	6	4	10	5
Expert #6	27.00	4	4	2	10	12
Expert #7	**3.00**	10	10	5	10	15
Expert #8						
Average	16.71	4.86	6.14	4.29	9.14	11.50
SD	7.65	3.18	2.61	2.69	1.95	10.29
Minimum	3.00	1.00	3.00	2.00	6.00	2.00
Maximum	27.00	10.00	10.00	10.00	12.00	30.00

Case #3: The Micro-Manager

Hrs/Week	Employee's Time	Manager's Time	HR's Time	Peers' Time	Subs' Time	Impact on Revenues
Expert #1	0.00	3	1	5	6	5
Expert #2	30.00	1	5	5	6	10
Expert #3	30.00	1	6	6	15	15
Expert #4	10.00	0	2	2	10	
Expert #5	20.00	1	1	1	15	2
Expert #6	20.00	1	1	2	20	5
Expert #7	20.00	2	5	3	15	15
Expert #8						
Average	18.57	1.29	3.00	3.43	12.43	8.67
SD	10.69	0.95	2.24	1.90	5.26	5.54
Minimum	0.00	0.00	1.00	1.00	6.00	2.00
Maximum	30.00	2.00	6.00	6.00	20.00	15.00

Case #4: The Victim

Hrs/Week	Employee's Time	Manager's Time	HR's Time	Peers' Time	Subs' Time	Impact on Revenues
Expert #1	4.00	3	6	1	1	2
Expert #2	4.00	3	4	4	3	20
Expert #3	10.00	6	10	10	10	15
Expert #4	8.00	3	4	3	5	5
Expert #5	20.00	1	4	1	8	2
Expert #6	13.00	8	10	4	20	30
Expert #7	10.00	5	6	5	5	10
Expert #8						
Average	9.86	4.14	6.29	4.00	7.43	12.00
SD	5.55	2.34	2.69	3.06	6.29	10.41
Minimum	4.00	1.00	4.00	1.00	1.00	2.00
Maximum	20.00	8.00	10.00	10.00	20.00	30.00

Case #5: The Techno-(wo)man

Hrs/Week	Employee's Time	Manager's Time	HR's Time	Peers' Time	Subs' Time	Impact on Revenues
Expert #1	2.00	10	6	10	15	5
Expert #2	20.00	5	1	10	2	30
Expert #3	2.00	4	6	4	8	30
Expert #4	0.00	0	1	2	3	0
Expert #5	20.00	0	4	0	15	10
Expert #6	13.00	4	2	2	10	50
Expert #7	3.00	10	3	8	8	15
Expert #8						
Average	8.57	4.71	3.29	5.14	8.71	20.00
SD	8.87	4.11	2.14	4.14	5.15	17.56
Minimum	0.00	0.00	1.00	0.00	2.00	0.00
Maximum	20.00	10.00	6.00	10.00	15.00	50.00

Here are definitions for items found in the following table:

Pay back (months): The return on training investment.

Salary All salaries should include the benefits package which usually amounts to 30% of base pay. Also include bonuses and commissions.

Revenue Responsibilities: This should approximate the total gross sales or production costs which the candidate affects by his actions.

Loss in Revenues: The approximate percentage of his influence on the preceeding number.

GLC program cost: A number which any organization may charge for development work for this employee.

Opportunity cost to company: While the employee is spending time off the job to take a program, what percent is lost to the company above his actual hours away? This is the cost of loss of leadership, inspiration or organization which the employee embodies while he is there. This percentage of time away is added to program duration hours in the formula to account for total program cost.

Sunk cost: The amount spent in one year or in the <u>duration</u> noted on this employee.

Burn rate: The monthly cost of maintaining this employee with current issues.

Replacement costs: The amount to acquire a new employee in that position.

Results of Sampling:
(Replacement costs not calculated)

Direct Cost	Ind #1	Ind #2	Ind #3	Ind #4	Ind #5	Ind #6
Number of people involved (#)	1	1	1	1	1	1
Yearly salary (including benefits)	$80,000	$100,000	$85,000	$100,000	$100,000	$80,000
Unproductive time (hrs/wk)		2	12.5		10	10
Duration of conflict (wks)	45	23	90	135	23	12
Total:	$0	$2,556	$53,125	$0	$12,778	$5,333
Intervention Cost						
Yearly salary (Including benefits)	$120,000		$60,000		$80,000	$80,000
Mgr salary ($/hr, incl. benefits)	$67	$0	$33	$0	$44	$44
Number of mgrs involved (#)	1		1		4	2
Unproductive time (hrs/wk/mgr)	2		3		2	1.5
Duration of intervention (wks)	45		45		12	12
Inappropriate solution ($)						
Total:	$6,000	$0	$4,500	$0	$4,267	$1,600
Replacement Cost						
Severance package ($)						
Vacant position ($)						
Search / Hiring ($)						
Training ($)						
Total:	$0	$0	$0	$0	$0	$0
Impact Cost (People)						
Peers (# people)					10	
Peer's salary ($/yr)					$100,000	
Subordinates (# people)	6	5	5	8	5	3
Subordinate's salary ($/hr)	$45,000	$60,000	$80,000	$70,000	$85,000	$60,000
Morale decay						
Poor role modeling						
Loss of creativity						
Loss of productivity	30.00%	5.00%	20.00%	30.00%	20.00%	5.00%
Total:	$81,000	$7,667	$160,000	$504,000	$145,667	$2,400
Impact Cost (Revenues)						
Revenues (Products & contracts)	$600,000		$900,000		$800,000	$100,000
Loss on revenues (%)	1%		10%		10%	3%
Outer world						
Total:	$6,000	$0	$180,000	$0	$40,889	$800
Total Cost						
Total	$93,000	$10,222	$397,625	$504,000	$203,600	$10,133
% of major player's salary	116%	10%	468%	504%	204%	13%
Burn Rate ($/wk)	$2,067	$444	$4,418	$3,733	$8,852	$844
Suggested Program						
Out-of-pocket program cost	$7,000	$12,000	$12,000	$15,000	$15,000	$9,000

Chapter Three

You May Recognize Some of These Folks!

To begin our study, we presented the following five composite cases to be evaluated in the exact form to follow. These five cases were invented particularly for this study so that each pattern could be quantified. We offered them to a dozen Silicon Valley executives who volunteered to assess the cases as though they were a part of their own jurisdiction. The cases are not to be confused with any real company or individual. Among the companies selected to help confirm our hypotheses were AMD, Intel, Lockheed Martin, Netscape, Raychem, Tandem, Xilinx and smaller and medium sized companies. We interviewed Human Resource professionals as well as experienced managers who were not familiar with the human resource approach to evaluating employees.

Each company assessed from its own internal values and perspective, but we could derive common generalities about each case. This led us to average hours lost depending on the behavior.

The costimator is like an easy income tax form. Each company or individual can plug in all their own numbers to derive the financial loss per individual situation.

Professionals whom we contacted were very cooperative about making estimates for examples of employees they work with every day. We are now using this formula for companies when they are not sure if the employee is worth the investment to get him help. Often managers are startled about the burn rate when they see the numbers. They may learn they are spending $10,000.00 a week on a dysfunctional behavior. These facts create a sense of urgency to make a "fix or sell" decision more quickly. There are times when, no matter what the burn rate, the employee has the key to a product or sales ingredient, so the company keeps him in spite of the cost.

These are the cases distributed to our sampling: In each of the following cases, the fictitious employee is critical to the company, the product or the sales function. Termination has been a consideration, but at this point, the decision-maker has chosen to maintain the employee in his current position.

Case One: The Intimidator

Company: **Aerospace, 2 billion in sales, 15 years blue chip, 7000 employees.** *Case*: **Vice President, Senior Legal Counsel, 11 years, 2 years current position, 7 peers, 6 direct reports.**

Will creates chaos wherever he goes. He publicly humiliates peers or staff with sarcastic barbs or judgmental statements. His general demeanor is negative although he proclaims that he believes he is funny. Three administrative assistants have left in the past years, while the one who remains seems to have the same impact on people as he does, yet she also complains about his abusive and demanding delegation style. People back away from him, but cannot always escape his aggressive comments in staff meetings where he seems to choose public criticism of others as a regular sport.

With the CEO he is more careful, but at a recent off-site, he pointed out a fatal logic flaw in the CEO's presentation in front of staff and major customers. The CEO's response was to ban Will from further meetings at that event.

This executive has been known to cause other employees to go home for two days. Sometimes, employees simply "forget" to go to a meeting which Will is scheduled to attend.   In the past six months, four of his direct reports and several of his key peer managers have spent four hour meetings discussing how to avoid his input and presence. The human resource group has spent many hours with disgruntled employees brainstorming about this man's behavior.

When Will is confronted, he becomes abusive and fault-finding with the messengers. He then refuses to cooperate with the current agenda in which he may be involved. This may last a day or two and then he appears to forget the conflict and proceeds as though nothing had happened. Others do not seem to forget.

Case Two: Stressor

*Company***: A progressive Software Company, 30 million in sales, 6 years old, 1200 employees. *Case:* Sales Director, reports to VP Sales, two years in current position. 5 peers, 7 direct reports.**

Margie is always running. She is stressed and she is a stress carrier. People around her feel anxious and dizzy. She is the subject of an average of three complaints a week, dispersed to her manager or human resource department. A variety of interventions have been employed, including a company-expensed trip to Hawaii, classes on stress management, and six or seven requests that Marg take a few days off at a time.

Turn-over in Margie's group is extraordinary, and absenteeism and special leaves are above average. Margie, of course, models severe workaholism: 16 hours a day, 6 days a week and complains that she never has time for her husband or her parents. She is habitually late, often holding up meetings because she alone has the sales notes for her staff and the largest customer. She speaks in long, hurried monologues and interrupts everyone. Her response modes are anger, aggravation, irritation and impatience.

Marge, however, spends hours discussing the latest slight by someone. When she does respond directly, it is with flaming e-mails or voice mails. She will call meetings after working hours to defend herself or tax others. Her reactionary style slows production and demoralizes her staff. She has little staff loyalty, while she protests about caring for her staff with expensive and inappropriate gifts.

Human Resources personnel meet regularly with another employee who complains about Margie. She has had several interventions presented to her, promises to take yet another yoga or meditation class, and seems to calm down for two days, maximum. When she receives notes or memos outlining her Type A behavior patterns, she retorts with: They don't know what they are talking about. This is the just the price for being a high performer—jealousy.

Case Three: Micro-manager:

Company: **Manufacturing, 24 million, 20 years old, 700 employees.** *Case*: **General Manager, reports to Vice President, Manufacturing, 12 years in company, 4 years in current position. 8 peers, 15 direct reports.**

George watches over everything. He has been asked to reduce his direct reports, but, in line with having to do it all himself, he does not want to delegate more authority. He holds four-hour staff meetings at close the of the day, Friday, which annoys his staff, and for which he will abide no absences. He asks for written and oral reports and he checks each item, line by line, in front of all his staff.

Additionally, George has one-on-one meetings for 15 hours of the week. No direct report attends an outside meeting with other departments without George's presence or permission. He must sign off on all requests over $5000, and he sits in on all initial interviews for new hires.

George's staff seems to be made up of "yes" people whose creativity is stifled. If he does maintain an innovative technical or strategic employee, he tends to over-tax him with details so significantly numerous that the new person eventually tends to miss the big picture. George requires so much minutia that employees become passive-aggressive.

George maintains the critical data for most products within his own domain. He inspects work that lead supervisors should do, and he requires extraordinary attention to detail from his staff members. No succession planning is discussed in his group, of course.

Case Four: The Withholder

Company: Semiconductor, 3 billion, 22 years, 12,000 employees. *Case*: Group Controller, reports to VP, Finance, 16 years, 5 years in current position. 12 peers, 5 direct reports.

Saundra, harried and overworked, is often forgotten when special meetings and events are called. Technically, she is the financial head of her product area, but her boss seems to conduct all group meetings and she is often subjected to preparing reports and handling the administrative tasks of her organization.

Saundra does not assume an assertive position and often ducks conflict. She believes that conflict is not a necessary element of the job, and she will simply miss a meeting if she believes she will be centered in a controversy. Of course, then, she often misses the coveted assignments.

She spends many hours a week in the office of the human resource specialist for her group, complaining about slights or insubordination by her reports, but she also feels a lack of trust from the HR group and will dismiss their suggestions with the notion that they may be setting her up to fail.

Saundra's employees do not feel empowered, often spending time in complaint sessions together, without Saundra, because they know she will not hear overt demands at meetings. They feel negative and will sabotage progress if they feel the action could indulge Saundra's victim stance.

Peers ignore Saundra, often finding themselves in a quandry because Saundra has important data necessary to draw a financial conclusion. They then have to re-do the work, and feel angry with Saundra. No one hesitates telling her when she delays the progress of a decision, to which Saundra mumbles, and then takes off for the afternoon to lick her corporate wounds.

Case Five: Techno-Bound Employee

Company: **Engineering Start-up recently Public, 15 million in sales, 4 years, 300 employees.** *Case*: **Vice President, Engineering, reports to CEO, President, 4 years with company and in current position. 4 peers, 7 direct reports.**

Mark is a brilliant technical innovator who designed the company's premier product. He has difficulty getting it produced because he spends time in the technical meetings and problem areas, and little time managing his people. He believes in hands-off management and does not even like to call his own staff meetings.

Mark meets one-on-one with his reports, but no communication passes between his people. He avoids conflict and will not bring to closure some elements of the work which interests his boss, the President, but for which he, Mark, has no interest. He does not push back with his boss, and does not facilitate disputes between his people. He often sends them off to work it out themselves when, in fact, they believe the decision should be his. Unless it is a technical decision, he is not interested.   Often this results in miscalculations by his team, poor morale, and missed deadlines due to multiple translations of a situation.

Mark ignores all training opportunities to improve his communication skills, and does not approve requests for leadership training for his staff. He does not allocate expenses for company events or parties. He will not tolerate or participate in small talk in the halls. He will select favorite technical people to spend hundreds of hours with, showing off, or exploring together, technical areas which interest him.

Mark does not approve of the marketing or sales managers and avoids the VP of finance. He discounts all of the VP's because they are not rational enough. He does respect the CEO/President, but complains that he does not have enough time with him. He skips all off-site meetings which could provide him with exposure to the president, by complaining that he would be wasting time with the other department heads.

More People and Behaviors You May Have Come to Love or Hate:

In case we've missed your favorite difficult employee, we've added a few more composites so you might recognize him or her. Only by identifying certain behaviors as red ink behaviors can an organization decide to make the appropriate moves to solve the problems. Although these cases are meant to be dramatic, we know you will recognize the employees around you whose subtle and insidious working styles often stifle growth and productivity.

The Causes and Solutions

In the following cases we attempted to look for root causes of the negative behavior, and then to present the solutions and specific interventions to begin the process of change. The samples are composites derived from our studies. These particular samples show the underlying causes of Red Ink Behavior.

Ivan, Legal Counsel

Ivan was young, handsome, spunky—and sought-after by many other competing organizations. Senior Legal Counsel and right-hand man for his president and for his blue chip 100 company, Ivan is the man of the hour—the torture hour! He swears, hits below the belt, and uses his incredible vocabulary for the last and killing word, particularly in public.

Ivan cannot understand why people are afraid of him. He thinks he is a good guy. He KNOWS he is, He also knows that deep down inside he is frightened and insecure sometimes, and he can't imagine that this part of him is not showing some of the time. He can't understand, then, why his timidity doesn't show through. He actually is more, much more, insecure than his behavior speaks. But no one knows this. He is always surprised that he is known as so intimidating.

Ivan rants and raves. He does this with great class. His vocabulary is vast and terminal. He wins battles and loses supporters with a turn of a terrible phrase. His incriminating and arrogant mouth has such a biting sound that colleagues shrink from his possible abuse.

Ivan, brilliant and fast thinking, seems to enjoy twisting the corporate knife in public. His prey will always be the one stumped by his vast repertoire and he usually has a fatal humorous entendre which can make the colleagues about the table snicker even while they cringe for the victim.

What are the costs of Ivan's testy ways? Lets start at the top with the President of the company. Since Ivan is on the senior staff and an important legal consultant to the president, he is involved in most company decisions. His president and company need him. He has a brilliant overview of the business world, his company's place in that world, and he makes the right calls most of the time.

He was referred to GLC, however, because finally even the president got tired of him. On an off-site in Malaysia, the president, John, finally became the victim of Ivan's redressing. With great drama and sarcasm, Ivan publicly, with a few customers in attendance, exposed some fatal flaws in the president's presentation. He didn't stop there. He took John aside and added more barbs. Ivan was on a roll. He drew the vice president of finance in and, again, in the presence of a small committee, managed the last aggressive and humiliating blast with the senior VP. Ivan was a tornado that weekend. However, his initial target, the president, finally balked.

"Clean up or get out," the president shouted at him the following Monday morning. Strangely, he had not observed the incriminating behavior which so many had complained about—until he became the target.

"And, don't let him in my sight until he is fixed," he growled to Ivan's boss. Ivan was devastated. He really admired John, cherished their relationship, and was chagrined to think that he might have been permanently disbarred from his senior circle.

What did Ivan's behavior cost the president and the company? Only one hour of the president's public time, but a dent in the sales cycle of the customer's response. The customer lost confidence in the president and delayed the buy for three long months. The on-going degradation for the company in the customer's eye is immeasurable, but we know it cost three months in that particular contract. And we know that cost to the company: a cool million. Further cost to the president is more difficult to calculate.

John, the president, went back to his hotel room, steaming. He called his wife about it. He daydreamed through the following morning's three hour meeting. He left the afternoon briefing, called his wife again, and took a long and frenetic nap in his room. Waking with a sour taste in his mouth, he then presided with the same sour demeanor through the planned celebration dinner. Ivan had intuitively ducked the dinner, but everyone was tense. The above are the one-time costs of that fateful weekend.

Other chronic and lower-level costs can be measured. The major damage did not occur on that one occasion. Ivan's aggressive and intimidating behavior was a regular event. At least once a week, he bullied someone. That someone would shrink away, have to digest the reaction, and then debrief with others about the explosion.

Each of these responses take time and rob creativity. A favorite hallway past-time is usually to talk about the Ivan-type tantrum. For victims of the tirade, the loss of productivity and the desire for and plotting for retribution can take several days at a time. We can calculate the victim's loss of productivity, multiply that by his hourly wage, and calculate the cost of one temper tantrum. We, of course, add in the lost time from peers and bosses who have to handle the complaints.

Further costs are accumulated by the acceleration of his staff's impotence when a staff meeting tantrum occurs. People come in stiffly, wary that their reports could induce the tantrum of the day. Innovation is stifled and interplay, which could be brainstorming, is curtailed while people are wary of the

demonstration of their "stupid" logic. Five of Ivan's direct
reports remain silent unless called upon. Two are not the least
bit intimidated by Ivan. In fact, they goad him on. When they
are targeted, they slough it off. But two other members leave
the room with ulcers burning in their stomachs, fearing the
next visit.

We did not calculate the ulcer costs. We did count a fifteen
minute loss of productive work for those two group members.
And, we did calculate the cost of turnover of three administrative assistants in the last year.

Well, what happened to Ivan? In an early session at GLC, we
interrupted him every time he said something snide or sarcastic. This happened fourteen times in a two hour session. We
called him on his value-laden words like "unconscionable" and
"vapid". There were twenty-five of them. "Stupid" hit the
paper eleven times.

The first thing we did with Ivan, however, was to build rapport.
We acknowledged his creative mind and intelligence quotient.
Later, we taught him about his emotional intelligence quotient
which was much, much lower. We noted his quick humor and
suggested it could be used in a new context. We also noted
that we knew this currently seemed impossible.

We then suggested that some underlying fear of his own might
be prompting his tirades. He resisted this notion with a very
high-minded delusion that, when people are stupid around him,
it is his duty to point that out. When we could convince him to
see his own interpersonal stupidity, he seemed to lighten up
somewhat. He was devastated to admit that people probably
laughed at him, not with him, and that he had no work friends
and ate lunch alone. His resistance and denial melted away

quite easily, since he was smart enough to see that he had only been indulging himself and that the cost to him was the CEO position he coveted—and much, much more.

To try to understand the possible root causes for Ivan's behavior, we've put together some causal percentages just to help illuminate his periodic and destructive working style. These are only hypothetical suggestions:

10%	Need for the spotlight at any cost
10%	Need for superiority over others
05%	Imprinted words and phrases from his father
25%	Reinforced sarcasm from prior thirty six years
20%	Habit triggered whenever an opportunity arose
05%	Current reinforcement about sarcasm
05%	Fear of being seen as an uninteresting wimp
20%	Fear of loss of control of others if they were not intimidated

100%

How does Ivan slink back into work now? Easily. He learned that only a 3% improvement is required and that gathering the awareness is 80% of the change task. He came to decide that you cannot make major moves to change unless you have integrated those changes into body, soul, and mind. With a few false starts and a couple of backslides, eventually Ivan decided that he wanted to be different. He realized he was in a stalemate in this company, but that he had also not progressed in maturity since his Ph.D. program.

Ivan found very creative ways to remind himself to hold back, clean up his harsh tongue, and look for ways to find people doing something right. Looking for positives in the behavior of those he did not understand was the hardest task of all. The critic in Ivan scared him away from easily complimenting others.

The immediate reinforcement for Ivan's 3% change was so dramatic that Ivan was quickly motivated to up his odds. People asked him what he had done: "Did you shave off your mustache? Did you get engaged? Did you win the lottery? Go to a health spa?" they asked.

Ivan did a brave thing in response to the questions. He told the truth. He explained his insight into his bad behavior and shared what he was doing about it. He even asked anyone who talked to him about it to give him feedback. This feedback loop eventuated in lunches, an invitation to go on his first California camping trip, and to the feeling of camaraderie which had evaded him his whole career.

Ivan took nearly a year to change his working behavior and nearly two years to change his reputation. He campaigned for himself: "I've been a jerk around here, my mouth has gotten me in trouble and I've caused a lot of unnecessary pain because I was an abusive show-off. At the expense of others, I was indulging myself. I don't want to do it anymore. Please call me on it if I start that high-road tirade again."

Ivan's last conquest was the president. He started with an e-mail, suggesting that he was grateful for the ultimatum and aware the he knew it might be awhile before the president trusted him again. John, the president, by the way, was cool about the first note, only answered in curt "wait and see" tones. He ignored Ivan for the better part of the next quarter. After three months, Ivan called the meeting and he was now authentic enough for John to believe his good intentions.

Ivan is now the company CEO.

Drew, the Project Manager

Drew had ninety five of the one hundred projects in the company's most significant division. He liked it that way. He also answered his own phone, wrote his own letters and did his own schedule. He had a very large span of control with twelve direct reports. He liked it that way. He worked an average of thirteen hours a day, six and one half days a week, and his family did not like it that way.

He was referred to Growth & Leadership Center because he was causing uproars with peers, and colleagues from other divisions found him inaccessible and very territorial. His boss, the company CEO, worried about a breakdown in Drew—a heart attack or perhaps, another form of burn-out. Drew's job was so all encompassing and he carried so much around in his head that everyone knew the company was in danger.

Arranging for the first meeting with Drew was a chore. Of course Drew was too busy—tasks too important to bother about Drew's health. Finally he staggered in, angry that he would have to take the time for such an outlandish activity as executive coaching.

By the way, in Drew's spare time, he also coaches his son's little league team. You can imagine the roster and game plan for those little eight year olds. Of course, this do-it-yourselfer did not need assistants or any parent helpers.

Drew was indignant about the company's worry and very fearful of giving up any of the control which he so fiercely held. Drew was in constant fear that one of his departments would be taken away. He honestly believed that, unless he held

on to the entire division, things would be unmanageable. We
know that he convinced himself because he could not cope
with the ambiguity of having some areas out of his direct
command. If he pulled every string, he was sure things would
go his way.

Drew's downfall was when one string got tangled with a
significant string in another division. The overlap pointed out
Drew's over-management of his division. In the seventh fight
for territorial technology, Drew went too far. It was reported
that his face burst into red, his veins extended in his forehead,
and in front of twenty people, Drew became "king baby",
ranting and shouting, and begging and losing it! "King baby"
is the executive on the throne who acts like a baby because,
without logic or appropriateness, he wants what he wants, even
when it is not available at any price!

The cost to the company of Drew's stronghold on decisions
finally exceeded his worth. He stifled other managers who took
out their frustrations in sabotaging techniques which cost the
company production time and moral decay. His subordinates
spent energy and time subversively trying to prove Drew was
wrong. They wasted company time with plots to trip up Drew.
The more timid employees just passive-aggressively continued
to be late for meetings, holding up progress, or forgot the
requested data or tasks. They always said yes to Drew. Then,
they always innocently concocted valid sounding excuses for
delaying completion of the task.

The calculation of missed assignment time for direct reports
was dramatic, but the ripple down effect of the employees
under Drew's direct reports was even more surprising. Without
power to act on their own, his men and women became
impotent to manage their people who, in turn, spent unproduc-

tive time complaining to each other, looking for ways to grab power back for their bosses, or fantasizing the demise of Drew, the dictator.

Drew's micro-control eroded the enthusiasm of the staff. The decline in innovation moved previously creative groups into whining organizations with employees looking for ways to get out of work. Simultaneously, Drew tried to pile more work on everyone.

He modeled overwhelm and overwork and most employees took extra sick leave. There were more cases of disability claims per capita in his department than in any other part of the company. The cost of malingering employees was noted by his human resource department.

Drew was fairly uncooperative when he worked with us. He wanted to complain about the company, his boss, and the imposition of having the possibility of sharing command. He could not understand why his boss wanted to distribute some of the work load. He did try some stress management techniques and, at least, began to see that he was losing his marriage with his over-controlling ways at home and at work.

Drew learned that he was dreadfully uncomfortable if he could not foresee the outcome of a specific situation. He became dysfunctional when he believed someone else might steer his boat for a time. He honestly believed that only he had the vision for this division and, if anyone grabbed a piece of the responsibility, things might go awry. To analyze the root antecedents of Drew's behavior we'll make some guesses at the distribution. These averages are taken from years of working with the controlling employee:

35% Fears of uncertain circumstances over which he
     has no control
20% History of command/control first boss or family
10% Inability to try new behaviors stemming from
     early ridicule
10% Ingrained habit of accepting responsibility (co-
     dependence)
25% Reinforcement from others who want to pass off
     responsibilities
     ___
100%

Just as Drew was evaluating the price of his high control, and GLC was struggling to help him to a reality test, his boss and the HR director conference called GLC to brainstorm how to tell Drew they would be walking him out the door in the next week.

They did walk him out the door. The division miraculously survived Drew's departure.

Drew went on to the next company, grabbing up responsibility again. His wife left him. His original company, our client, thanked us for preparing Drew to receive feedback. We felt we had failed. We always want the employee to make the appropriate changes to save his career and his life. When we finally calculated the cost to the company of Drew's ownership issues, we believed we had done the company a favor.

Two months later, Drew came to us—voluntarily. He had cut all company ties, but he wanted to thank us for waking him up about his "do-it-yourself-ism." He swore he would learn to delegate and he told us that he now shared his new little league coaching program. We were not confident that, without constant maintenance, Drew would not lapse back to his responsibility fetish. Currently, Drew is working into the night in his new job. He claims he is watching his control-drives. We still worry.

Tanya, National Sales

Tanya, Type A Behavior executive, danced into our office, papers and her shirt tails flying. She jubilantly congratulated us on our company and on herself for agreeing to do this coaching program. She rapidly began talking for the first fifteen minutes without pausing for a breath.

We learned that she was the top saleswoman, a director in her fast-growing dynamo company. We learned that she had a son, aged two, a nanny, and a husband who also traveled. She was far ahead of everyone in her department. She boasted that she rarely fraternized with anyone in her department except her boss, a senior vice president who continued to reward her with raises and perks.

When Tanya let down, though that means take a breath—she began to cry, claiming she was just about to quit her marvelous job. "I'm shaking every night, can't sleep, I'm cross with my baby, and I'm anxious about everything. If I am not at work and at the buzz saw, I am home, laying on my bed, paralyzed. I can't do anything at home and my paperwork piles up constantly. Sometimes I just throw the paperwork away. It hasn't hurt me too much yet, but I have missed a few travel reimbursements. The worst part is that everyone else in our group hates me."

The cost to the company was Tanya's inconsistency. If she left the company, she would create a big chasm and no one was talking succession planning. Tanya was, by the way, just talking. She is a typical Type A with a talking stream of consciousness, bouncing from topic to topic, and interrupting us if we tried to insert an idea.

Another loss of productivity cost would occur when Tanya translated the actions of her boss or others to be one of the common Type A behavior pattern disturbances. She would claim the four I's of this pattern: Interference, Injustice, Injury, and Insult, both simultaneously and serially. Here are some of Tanya's complaints:

#1. Interference: The sales staff would interfere with her progress by not working hard enough or preparing her materials accurately. The staffs translation, however, was that Tanya was a procrastinator who waited until the last moment to throw things at them in rough and incorrect forms, flaming with mistakes she expected the staff to catch.

#2. Injustice: The boss would be unfair by moving her territory around or asking her to train new people. She would lose sleep and productivity over her translation of this injustice, instead of understanding that this may be one of the sales dilemmas in every sales organization. Instead, she took it personally.

#3. Injury (the third hallmark of a Type A behavioral pattern): Because Tanya was so outgoing and yet thin-skinned, she would create high emotional upset when she believed she was insulted. In her frame of reference and, because she tried so hard to compliment and notice everyone, she could become enraged over a minor slight. The range of insults went from the seating arrangement at a dinner party to the commission disbursements, even though she led the pack on financial rewards.

#4. Insult: The fourth translation of intentions of others by Type A people is that they assume someone tried to make them look bad or ridiculous. Their worry about looking good overtakes the good judgment which would allow them a more benign translation of the intentions of others.

The most prevalent and destructive sign of a Type A behavior pattern is hidden hostility. Under all of Tanya's words and busy and frantic actions, was the possibility that she could light up at any moment. "Closet A's" internalize this anger permanently, only showing minor episodes of rage if pushed to the limit of endurance. Tanya, a raging A, was prone to venting her responses to others quite easily. The possibility of Tanya's anger, without notice or apparent provocation, would keep employees and colleagues in a tentative position, not allowing the full range of strategic or tactical maneuvers to be explored and, thus costing the company a great deal of unproductive time.

Because Tanya fervently wanted to be accepted, she chose to listen to our suggestions. She caught herself interrupting and learned to listen and then to reflect the other's perceptions before she burst into her answer. With more reflective time available, Tanya took off her blinders and decided to try some of the practice drills we proposed. She learned to drive in the slow lane, to avoid working while flying on airplanes, and to try not to do three things at once. She learned to eat without doing anything else. That was a big challenge. She also learned to listen when her boss talked, without preparing her answer or her defense.

Tanya's major hurdle was to give up the hostility which whirled about her. Consciously she had to reformat each negative event into a possible positive outcome. Eventually this translation became unconscious, and our pessimist became optimistic even in the face of a sales "No".

Tanya sent her support staff to us to develop a common vocabulary and to create a feedback loop so that she could be reminded if she slipped. Others learned of their Type A patterns (Type A's are attracted to other A's). Eventually, Tanya built 25% reflection time into her life. This allowed her to plan, contemplate, celebrate and to anticipate.

On her last visit, Tanya sauntered into our office in a leisurely way, offered up a bouquet of flowers for our male coach, and did not even notice that she was on time, giving up the chronic lateness common to those who think they have so much to do in so little time. Tanya graduated with honors.

Dan, the Engineer

Dan, the facts man, was confused. He was referred to GLC because he could not seem to collaborate. He believed that he was very cooperative and he felt hurt that a nice guy like him could be perceived as a non-team player. A very credentialled engineer in a senior position. Dan thought of himself as the consummate consensus builder. He also believed in and utilized the "disagree and commit anyway practice".

Dan's blind spot appeared when he realized that he only collaborated when he believed the right areas were being addressed. His data had to match another's data before he would consider agreement and he did not get to the "disagree and commit anyway" stage if the data points were not aligned.

Dan had never heard of *meta messages* or *process versus content*. He had been through many leadership courses and liked the trendy MBA books, but he honestly had never considered that the method of delivery of the data counted at all. The facts were inviolate.

We did perception exercises which proved that perception can color the translation of some facts. Dan was surprised that he could have been missing out on some obvious facts about his own distorted version of events. He realized that when he was put in a position of crisis, with distraction, and multiple agendas presented in a very simple team exercise, he was not reliable. We surmised that he learned at that moment, that he was also just a human being.

When we could logically point out that he might be missing some opportunities for collaboration and effective group thinking because of his own stubborn approach to his facts, he yielded and listened.

The cost of Dan's compulsive data-gathering style was high. He turned off other colleagues and he had certainly never learned to "manage up". His boss put off giving Dan important assignments because he did not have the energy to argue at every turn. Dan would aggressively pursue a subject, often to prove he was right or that his approach was right, long after the subject was no longer relevant.

Dan was not good at rapport-building with others, rarely showed a light approach, and seemed to want the facts much more than he wanted a team approach. His peers excluded him from meetings, which then created a need for further meetings with his subordinates to get the tasks done.

The cost of HR and his management team's intervention on Dan was horrendous because Dan was a confusing character. He was a nice man. He meant well. He was polite and courteous and never raised his voice. His HR group would meet for hours trying to think of a proper intervention for Dan. His reviews were always good. Unfortunately in the past, his company had not rated him on interpersonal team-building. Each time people would meet to discuss him, they would shake their heads and plan another 360 degree review for Dan.

The expensive price to the company was the cost for Dan's subordinates. Unless they had a justified and rational approach to a problem, Dan could not relate. Even when they had a logical approach to a problem, if it did not align with his concerns in the problem, he would change the subject. If the data points did not intersect, he would become obsessed with his vision of the problem. His subordinates would go away, disappointed and often taking off in the wrong direction because they could not understand Dan.

Dan, the eternal student, listened well to our suggestions. First we taught him *Reflective Listening*, which is the kind of listening in which you do not answer first, but attempt to let the other person know that you understand his perception. He could not learn it. He balked. He got sullen. He wanted out. Then we explained that he didn't have to agree with what the other person said; only to acknowledge that he understood what he or she was saying. Then he began to really listen. In practice, I told him that I could no longer meet with him because the room was painted purple and I was beginning to have a headache. I got quite emotional about the color of the room. We saw Dan almost turning purple himself as he finally gasped out, "Well, since you are experiencing this room as purple, I can see why you can't continue the session."

Dan learned to bridge other people's feelings and agendas. We taught him that emotional intelligence is composed of four components: the ability to soothe oneself, to channel anger appropriately, to delay gratification, and to know one's impact on others. When Dan could give up his belief that there was only the truth to worry about, he began to relate to others. Collaboration became easy. He even headed a team-building session, expounding on learning each other's working style differences.

Why Dan held on to data-driven conversations so long:

30%	Dan's history of rewards for his focus on facts
20%	His technology required accuracy and preciseness
20%	Blind to his obstinacy and deaf to feedback
30%	No compelling reason to change until job threatened

100%

Dan was an example of a quiet leak which drained company funds and company goodwill. Communication was bleak and non-existent even for other engineers because Dan had no capacity to relate beyond the facts of a project.

The bonus for Dan's changes were visible in some group experiments where he was praised for his humanity and sensitivity. This gave him the courage to seek a relationship for the first time in his fifty-six years. Thankfully, Dan married a librarian.

Paula, the Entrepreneur

Paula, the perfectionist, owns her own small company, the Browning Telescope Company. She is the prototype entrepreneur, ready to do anything for the good of the company. Unfortunately, she is also the entrepreneur prototype who starts a business because he or she is convinced that the technology the company is founded on is sound.

Paula is right that the telescope is magnificent. She wants the forty-four thousandth one to look and sound and feel like the fourteenth one she made years earlier. Unfortunately, again, Paula does not have the pragmatic and realistic approach that so many entrepreneurs eventually must adopt about their companies and their products.

Paula was self referred, having heard GLC's Founder speak at an owners meeting. She was ready to work and motivated to do whatever it takes to maintain her currently mutiny-bound staff. "Whatever": that is the dilemma. "Whatever" included giving up perfectionism. This was a big leap for Paula.

The first step in the GLC program was to assist Paula in accepting that she was about to lose her company if she did not take dramatic steps. Her perfectionism had cost employees, morale, and finally, customer satisfaction.

Paula had to sign every letter, every invoice, every production write-off, every agreement, and then she had to personally inspect each aspect of the telescope components. Employees (there were one hundred of them) were leaving because they had no sense of work satisfaction. Paula was her own one person Quality Assurance department. Her personal inspections were not profitable. Since the company had a handsome profit sharing plan, Paula would pull something off the line, causing re-work issues which the lead supervisor did not think were worth the delay and re-routing.

Paula was a perfectionist with her administrative staff as well. Each typographical error seemed to provide an opportunity for Paula to reconfigure the whole system on a particular document. When a department planned an off-site meeting, even though the budget had been approved by Paula, the line items needed her stamp. She took a day off work to personally visit the site, finally vetoing it because the cafeteria system looked unkempt. It was only a one day affair for twenty-two people and they liked the rustic style of the facility. They would have lived through unwashed apples.

Paula represents costly management errors in judgment. Her organization is no longer a custom shop and some re-work due to customer complaint is necessary given her shipping numbers. Supervisors begged for a quality control department. Secretaries urged Paula to stay away from their letters, and janitors shuddered when she strolled in on their night-time cleaning.

First we explored with Paula her own need for perfection. It had been drummed into her head from her first boss, and long before that. Paula remembers being a three year old who sorted her toys by color and size. This attention to detail paid off when she shipped her first telescopes. But telescope eye pieces are not perfect. They contribute spherical and chromatic aberrations and distortions to the final image. Focal ratio was Paula's byword. She seemed unwilling to give up the ratio that planetary and lunar viewing requires for less than perfect central image sharpness.

We calculated the down time from Paula's idiosyncrasies.
Then we added in her disgruntled employee's downtime when
he storms and fumes around the office. We also added the
downtime in others who sympathetically listen to and concur
with his complaints. The total loss in productivity astounded
Paula.

Giving up perfectionism meant that she did not have to over-
correct to zero, but needed to determine, with priority systems,
when she had a right to stop production. We drew the *important* versus *urgent* matrix and urged Paula to quantify each area
of concern for her. We asked her to assume that errors came
with the territory and implementing a customer service
department far outweighed the cost of the Paula trauma.

In order to re-establish credibility, Paula called an all-hands
meeting and suggested that some new era policies would be
established. Her "management by walking around" would be
replaced with thoughtful and visionary planning to double the
business within the year. She asked for employee patience and
installed a safeguard system for when Paula slipped and caused
chaos on the floor. She showed a few of our coach-experts off
to her staff, to prove she was serious. She then established a
maintenance review for herself to assure she was being faithful
to her more relaxed management style.

Paula still lost her plant manager. His replacement dipped into
the net sales picture. It also created other shaky employees.
She got serious, though, and dramatically and vigorously went
about proving her changes to the whole staff. She wanted them
to know the changes would be permanent She scratched her
name off many sign-off documents and re-routed areas to avoid
being in the loop. She saved her company, her senior staff, and

the financial strain her impositions had caused the entire organization.

Possible root causes of Paula's perfectionism:

35%	A belief system which generalized "perfect" to every aspect of the business
15%	Concern that there were no other redeeming factors to sell about her product
40%	Worry that she could not give up the obsessive thinking and planning
10%	No accumulation of "letting go" tools and consciousness raising about impact

100%

Paula keeps sending employees to our programs. She can spot a perfectionist easily now and talks to them about cluttered minds needing uncluttered surroundings. She believes that she is no longer beleaguered by anxieties and fears that she or the company were not enough. She knows she is good enough. Thats good enough!

Conrad, Marketing Director

Conrad, the critic, comes in many forms. This Conrad was in marketing, a senior officer, and a great guy! People thought he was very smart, appreciated his dedication, and resisted every opportunity to be with Conrad in any team meetings!

Conrad could not brainstorm. He actually feared that, if a liberal or radical idea was tossed about too long, people could settle on this notion. He had been reinforced for

pointing out errors in judgment, logic, and certainty, indeed, for most of his finger-pointing life. Conrad had a moral fiber which judgmentally labeled anyone who was forsaking his notion of quality or ethics. This high-mindedness stifled creativity and stopped progress in planning and crisis meetings.

Conrad was not discriminating about error identification. A big budget error got as much play from him as an estimate number on a rough draft flow chart. If something made it to a paper, he believed it was biblical and, therefore, should be accurate.

Let's start with Conrad's team of ten reports and a full staff of eighty-eight people. Each time he encountered someone, he believed it was his duty to parent them by pointing out problems. He did not engender solutions—only uncovered the problems. "When someone does the job right, I don't have to applaud them. That is what he is getting paid for," he said.

Conrad was motivated by his own internal judge who decided if he did something well or not. The judge was quite unforgiving and difficult, but Conrad was used to high performance. Since he disdained praise or rewards from anyone else, even his boss, he could not understand those who needed a pat on the back from him.

"Dismissables" we call them at GLC. These are the victim employees who are thrown away by critics like Conrad. He disposed of many colleagues as "dismissables" because they did not have his high standards for quality. He considered them incompetent and would try to work around them, certainly never seeking their counsel for anything Conrad deemed important. These "dismissables" became cost factors for the company. Each time they were left out of the communication loop, they cost the company time and energy.

When we calculated Conrad's list of "dismissables", multiplying them by occurrences by year, by their salary, by the hours lost, the **Red Ink** flowed. The trickle down effect, of course, meant that, if an engineering manager was on Conrad's black list, his people missed information, and set off on foreign courses. They also felt great confusion, if not rancor, when they later learned that Conrad had the data and could have prevented the stress and consequences.

The critic usually starts young. He may notice his parents or siblings in error, and is then reinforced by a parent who is also a critic. They espouse the theory that if your family can't tell you, who can? The critic does very well in school. Others hate to have Conrad grading their papers, but teachers love him When he points out errors on the board, the teacher may not love him as much, but the other students move Conrad up a notch because he humiliated the teacher. He takes his strokes wherever he can.

The Conrads of the world do well in graduate school, often ending up as a teacher's aids. Tired professors will let Conrads do all the work, find all the errors, and they give them many strokes for their efficiency. This even works very well in early professional careers. The new employee seems really sharp when he or she points something out in a staff meeting. People notice the critic until they become the recipient of the criticism.

Conrad's cost to the company is exponential. Each layer of management begins to resent him for past humiliations and they strive to get Conrad. This is not easy to do. Conrad has guarded himself for a life-time. His job is to be the judge, not the defendant He stays on the offense. Defense is left to his opponents who spend a weekend writing the rebuttals to Conrad, even when it is not a priority item they may be debating.

Employees who work with Conrad learn to take orders, not to think independently. The innovative employees move on, looking for opportunities to explore and grow. The less creative folks stay, but they get cold. There are no warm rewards from Conrad and, we know that unless there are some intangible reinforcements for most employees (Conrads are the exception), employees shrivel away.

Much like the do-it-your-selfer and the perfectionist, Conrad marches to his own drum. Unless he is running the company, he is subject to the collaborative thrust of the peer population. His teams stay unimaginative and defensive He stifles vision. In this company, his CEO shivers when Conrad enters the room. The boss loves to send him off to explore an appointed dilemma (usually found by Conrad) so that the rest of the meeting can proceed without the wet blanket tossed upon some very hot ideas.

In the GLC program, Conrad proceeded to discover errors of omission and detailed mistakes in our concepts or our written materials. Coaches switched, and, in case consultation about Conrad, a unanimous groan followed his name at every case call. But we persevered because we know that, down deep inside Conrad is a scared little kid who is wary about being exposed if he does not have everything right.

One of our Conrad types talked about his mother, a lawyer, who required the right answer from him for every question asked. The consequence for a wrong answer or no answer at all was always a ruler on the knuckles. So Conrad strove for answers. His immediate reflex was to always get the answer. He could not understand why others were more lax in their preparation.

Catching someone doing something right was difficult for Conrad, but when he decided that his job depended on it, he set out to find something right to comment upon. Surprisingly, it was not too hard.

A more difficult assignment was asking Conrad to look for an approximation of success from someone and reward it. "But the job is not done," he would wail. "She only did it once in five reports," he would explain. When Conrad mastered learning theory, and began a process of positive reinforcement for even approximations of success, his people starting asking his opinion again. As homework he was asked to give two positives for every critical comment to a colleague. Being the good student, he tried. We began to praise him, and, surprisingly, he discovered he liked this.

When Conrad trusted us completely, we reminded him about the first visits and how discouraging it was to have him point out the faults in our work even before he gave us a try. We talked about our own motivation level, and wondered out loud with him about the motivation level of his own staff. Conrad got the message. He knew he had to over-correct for awhile. That's why his testimony is so flowery: "GLC showed me why I was not successfully motivating anyone to work with me. They changed my life and saved a career for a misguided, struggling, conscientious guy who never could have figured this out for himself. I was too busy pointing out the other guy's mistakes."

Chapter Four

Timely Interventions

Problem employees seem to be the last to learn about their difficult behaviors. By the time they get to our office they are shocked and surprised about the magnitude of their problems. They are often humiliated as well. Why does this happen?

The difficult employee is hard to approach. He stays in denial about his working habits or rationalizes them with past successes using some of the same behaviors. He also quotes the CEO or President who models the same kind of style, but seems to pull it off better. A results-first company we work with has a culture modeled by the CEO who may be a bit of a tyrant, but is also known as a visionary and he's brilliant. He can pull it off. Our identified participant can't.

Because the boss or human relations officer or his peers can't get through, the problem festers and the consequences continue to mount. Faced with such a situation, the tendency for the

organization is to let itself overheat and allow the difficult one
to under-perform until the toll far exceeds any reasonable level
of pain and suffering. The real cost is in lost productivity.

Another serious problem also occurs. Often the very best
employees, who won't put up with this behavior, leave the
department or the company. This is the last thing a company
wants, to lose excellent people because of abuse from marginal
people.

The identified problem person does not take feedback easily.
He may erupt with defensiveness. The timid shy away.
Others say he is not worth it. They won't invest. Another
response is the interrogation. Our difficult person is in so
much denial and has mastered the defense of rationalization so
well that the messenger must be as rational and logical as he is
to complete the feedback.

Timely interventions often hurt. They are hard to deliver.
They are not well received and they are usually too late. If you
feel the resentment mounting as you approach his or her office,
you can be assured that it is already very late. The final
consequence to the difficult person is the ultimate humiliation
of being the last to know about his notorious behavior.

The following case studies suggest the cost of late interventions. The names have been changed to protect confidentiality.
What remains are the relevant behaviors and the cost impacts
of **not taking action**.

Jim

Jim was a senior executive in a large and very well known high
tech company in Silicon Valley. Bright and articulate, Jim had
been with the company for 16 years. His company loyalty was

unquestionable and his knowledge was considered to be well worth his nearly $1 million annual compensation.

There were flaws in Jim's style that were causing the company to take a look at whether Jim should remain with the company. His peers and subordinates could not stand Jim's behavior. They found him nearly impossible to relate to. They agreed that he was extremely intelligent but also felt that he cared little for anything except his own agenda and goals. He had to be right in every encounter.

The outward symptoms were fairly clear. When Jim listened to someone, there was never a smile or a nod of the head, or any sign that he was really taking it in. He would sit stonefaced. Often he would interrupt a person in mid-sentence when he felt he had heard enough. He would stare through you as though you were transparent with eyes that seemed to perpetually glare. His statements tended to be in absolutes leaving little room for debate.

While Jim's ideas were usually good and in the company's interest, no one wanted anything to do with him. It was a lose-win situation for all that worked with him, i.e., they would come away feeling they always lost and Jim would always win. It was not an understatement to say that his colleagues and reports hated him. Further, they didn't trust him and, for the most part, would have been delighted at his demise.

The situation had gone on for years with little or no attempt at intervention. Jim had been told that his style was difficult for people but he had no idea what that really meant or what he could do about it. For him, his behavior was perfectly rational. For him, it was a blind spot.

After 16 years of Jim on the job, GLC was asked to help with an executive coaching program. Within three months, the transformation was essentially complete. After the initial shock of learning how unpopular he had become, or how little respect, influence and trust he had in the organization, Jim worked hard to understand his impact on others.

Jim began to remind his face to respond along with his brain. He began to listen with his eyes, giving appropriate attention to the speaker. He practiced showing vulnerability and admitted when he caught himself interrogating instead of listening for the other person's perspective. Jim gained clarity on his behaviors and the impact they had on others. He was given the skill sets to enable change and the drill and practice to convert them into comfortable habits. **The productivity drain of 16 years was reversed in 3 months.**

Costimator Analysis for Jim Blackstone:

Cost of not taking action $350,000 per year.
Cost of fixing the problems $ 24,000 over a three
                                          month period

David

David is president and general manager of a Silicon Valley electronics company, a major subsidiary of an eastern con-glomerate. Within his subsidiary, he is the top executive with P&L responsibility and considerable autonomy. On his monthly trips to the parent company, he became a peer to other subsidiary presidents and a subordinate to the big boss.

David had a style marked by directness, animation, and a tendency to react to pressure by raging at those around him.

He had a forceful personality that was intimidating to most of his subordinates. His VP direct reports were capable but without much opportunity to think beyond their compartmentalized departments.

The key decisions, although discussed in executive meetings as group decisions, were really decisions that David had already reached. He would bring a topic up for discussion and manipulate the group until they had reached his conclusion. The executives understood the reality and quietly withdrew their initiatives, creativity, and sense of responsibility. They looked at their jobs as strictly running the details within their respective departments.

The chronic problem was impacting the effectiveness of virtually everyone in the company. Finally, at the courageous urging of his HR director, David recognized that he had serious blind spots that were getting in his way. He referred himself to GLC for executive coaching.

It wasn't long before we discovered one of the root issues. David had a belief that was very deep and very limiting. It was a control issue. Although viewed as a strong manager, he was deathly afraid of going into any meeting where the outcome was uncertain. He would go out of his way to gather data and arrive at the answer before any meeting. For him, the object was then to steer the group decision toward his conclusion. To do otherwise, he reasoned (believed) was to face total loss of control and be put in a situation of complete inadequacy.

As David began to see the impact of his behavior, he became interested in learning alternative styles. We equipped him with the skills, and even gave him the words to say in certain situations. We helped him establish the means of self-correction for the inevitable slips into old patterns.

Costimator Analysis for David Brentley:

Cost of not taking action	$250,000 per year
Cost 4 mo. of fixing the problems	$ 12,000 total

In David's case, the three year total cost of not taking action was a staggering $750,000. In business terms, the cost of fixing the problem represented only a $12,000 investment! The return on investment, in Costimator terms, was much higher than ordinary. Add to this the enormous relief by the collective subordinate group at the transformation in their leader. After the fact, the only wish was that **timely intervention** had occurred much earlier.

Why Do Managers or HR Professionals Hesitate?

It is nearly impossible to give critical feedback without repercussions. No one likes to hear bad news about himself, so delivering negative news is usually accompanied by blaming, defending, anger or sadness. Most of us do not want to make others uncomfortable. Therefore, we hesitate to take action in unpleasant situations.

We also hesitate because we know that we are not perfect either. We place ourselves in the other person's shoes and we know that we would not like to hear that our behaviors are too expensive for the company.

Last of all, the legal ramifications of wrongful termination have handcuffed some routine complaints and consequences. It is hard to feel secure about action when the manifestation of the human behaviors are so complex and cumbersome.

The examples in this book are an attempt to give the reader insight into the fact that there are some habits and working styles which are very destructive to the big picture in an organization.

The best direction is to err on the side of trying an intervention with the caveat that you are simply attempting to help the employee. In nearly all cases, you are. Some attempts to assist are clumsy and awkward, and others don't work at all, but our suggestion is that you give it round one. When round one fails, try again. Acknowledge the failure, and give it several more attempts. The employee, the situation, may be worth it.

Timely interventions can occur when behavior is first noticed. This means taking the risk early when you may not even be sure if the behavior is chronic or once-in-a-lifetime. When you are uncertain about what Martha said to a fellow employee, begin with, "Martha, I'm not sure I'm on the right track on this, but it appeared that you publicly humiliated Ruth at that last meeting. Was that an accident or your intention.? If it was your intention, I'd like to tell you how I felt about it. Maybe our team- mates might have also had that reaction. Do you want to create this concern in others?"

If the problem person is not in your domain, but he or she affects someone for whom you are responsible, start coaching. Suggest that it won't be easy and that you will be a sounding or practice board, and that you will help strategize the approach. Don't be like the manager who proudly told us that he threw two twenty dollar bills at two feuding subordinates, and suggested, "Go have lunch and come back fixed or you are both fired!"

A foolproof approach is simply to ask permission to give feedback. "This may not be my business, and I may be wrong, but I'd like to give you some feedback which might help in your approach with that customer. Would you be willing to listen?"

Then, expect that even with approval, he or she will interrupt you with rational reasons for the behavior. Be a good listener and reflect his or her logic. Then proceed with, "I'd like to give you another perspective. May I? Because what you are doing doesn't seem to be accomplishing what you want."

Give yourself a pat on the back when you make a timely intervention. It is never easy. People don't remember to thank you later either. You may change their lives, their families and work colleagues around them, and the appreciation could be late or sparse. You are, however, doing your job making things and people work!

Chapter Five

From Red Ink to Black Ink Success Stories

When a company or organization can discover just how costly the named *Red Ink Behaviors* can be, they are sometimes willing to make the moves to change an employee's actions. The skills and drills are quite simple. The understanding of the behavior and its impact on others will be the most important task for the employee.

In the year of 1996, our company, GLC, was in some way responsible for the appointment of three out of the dozen new Vice Presidents in a large semi-conductor company. Each of these executives had been a director who could not seem to get to the next level. Each was an incredible performer who was underused and under-appreciated because of some observable and pesky Red Ink Behaviors.

We sometimes see the recipient of feedback take the corrective action on his own. We want to close this book with some success stories which might exemplify the changes from *red to black ink* for the companies and employees who risked change. These last examples demonstrate the optimism we have for turning red ink to black.

Gabriel

Gabriel believed he was funny. People laughed at his jokes. People also laughed *at* him. He didn't know this, though. They laughed at him, behind his back, before he walked into the room, or after he had adjourned a meeting.

Gabriel was VP of Sales, a sarcastic and intimidating guy who earned, with bonuses, a million dollars a year. He had six expensive direct reports and five peers, all of whom tried to avoid being around Gabe as much as they could.

Why couldn't anyone tell Gabe the truth? Why did his annual reviews down-play his biting tongue? He was as sarcastic as Don Rickles. He was the resident cynic who could be as sardonic as possible. He had an escalating style if you attempted to prove your point. When he was angry or in a crisis, the bite was too frightening for anyone in his 13,000 employee company to debate. Oh, the President might have. Gabe was only Vice President of Sales. But his numbers were too high, his sales too critical to the success of the company, and the president was too conflict-avoidant to be willing to face the wrath of Gabriel. And so the company endured.

When he volunteered to come to our center, his company and our company were dumbfounded. He came because he received a poor review from someone he respected, and some gentle feedback from his subordinates. No one had mentioned his sarcasm. We did...

Gabriel protested that if he were to give up his sarcasm he would have nothing left. It is common to worry that when we are asked to alter our basic personality traits we believe there may be nothing left. There are no workable styles to replace those front-runner habits. "I'm not really sarcastic; I'm funny," he mused. We did not back down.

We explained that he was hurtful, abusive and that he cut off creativity in others. We played back many possible scenarios in which Gabe probably halted productive thinking because others were frightened that he would zap them. He learned that although his intention may have been noble, his reputation was now overwhelming. He had repair work to do. Yet, Gabe could not imagine giving up his **signature trait.**

When we explored the roots of the trait, it was clear his family communicated by kidding each other. No one told their honest feelings. Those around him were applauded for being cuttingly funny. The deeper the cut, the more the applause. This communication style saw Gabe through high school and the debate team, college and the debate team, and finally the first 15 years of his successful career in the semi-conductor business. He had no idea how to give up the sarcasm.

We gave him a difficult assignment: one full week of no humor at all. We urged him to be bland, boring and quiet. And we urged him to smile a lot. He was incensed. He thought this inane behavior would cause people to believe he was ill. He thought all meetings would be dreary. And, most of all, he thought he couldn't do it.

He did it. He returned a week later with a big smile on his face. "Well," he started, "they asked me all week what was different about me. They thought I had shaved my mustache off (never had one), or that I had gone to a spa, or I had a major and wonderful secret. They also thought I looked so darned relaxed," he boasted.

Amazingly, it wasn't hard. Of course he had promised to practice this at home too, with a wife and two teen-aged sons whom he had been molding in his own image. Instead of the dinner table bantering, Gabriel started telling the truth. He told his sons about his bad review and what people really thought about him. There was no time for quips because the boys were too busy telling him the truth about how frightening family dinners used to be. One son had tried to keeping up with his dad, but his friends were fed up with his sick humor. The other son gave up and rarely spoke up at home.

Gabe didn't think he could keep it up, but the positive feedback he received reinforced his desire to tone down his repertoire of negative comments. He learned he could be vulnerable and even bored without nailing someone else. People came to him for advice and shared confidences they had never shared before. Gabe quickly realized that a less biting approach won him the appreciation and support he was looking for.

As a part of our program, Gabe was asked to do an advertising campaign about his changes. It was the company president who gave him the most profound feedback after Gabe explained what he was doing. "Gabe, I've been wary of you from the first day we met. In the last five years when you wanted me to go to conferences or on customer calls with you. I always begged out. To be honest, I was afraid you would humiliate me with some joke at my expense. I always felt slow around you, and the anxiety over being humiliated made me even slower."

Gabe still slips, but everyone is urged to let him know when he does. He has dredged up some clean and non-toxic humor and he still loves to laugh. Now the company laughs with him. We added the cost of delays caused by employees who were unwilling to risk approaching Gabe collaboratively to the cost of time wasted by employees who were angry and stifled by Gabe's humiliating jibes. To this we added the potential of lost business opportunities resulting from his boss's unwillingness to meet with customers or accompany him to conferences.

Gabe's benefits and salary (totaling nearly a million dollars) plus the costs of his Red Ink behavior far exceeded his gross sales contribution to the company. Now, of course, Gabe is a financial asset. He likes himself more. His subordinates and peers are relaxed. He was just promoted to senior vice president, one of three. And nobody is laughing.

Costimator for Gabriel:

GLC Red Ink Behavior   -   Costimator Analysis

Please supply the following information:	ID:	49

* Include all benefits in salaries (e.g., stocks, bonuses, insurances, etc...)

Last:		First:	Gabe	Company	XYZ
Title:	VP Sales				
Problem Description:	Sarcastic / Intimidating				

Salary ($K/yr)*:	1000	Severance package ($K):		800
DEP's lost hours/week:	1	Search hiring ($K):		330
Problem duration (Mo):	12	Training ($K):		26
Direct Cost:	**$25,000**	**Replacement Cost:**	**$1,156,000**	

Manager's sal ($K/yr)*:	1200	HR person's sal ($K/yr)*:		75
Manager's lost hrs/wk:	0.25	HR person's lost hrs/wk:		3
Dur.of intervention (Mo):	3	Other persons ($K/wk):		0
	Intervention Cost:	**$3,281**		

Number of peers:	5	Number of subordinates:		6
Peers' salary ($K/yr)*:	800	Subordinates' salary ($K/yr)*:		400
Peers' lost hrs/wk:	3	Subordinates' lost hrs/wk:		4
	Impact Cost (People):	**$540,000**		

Revenues responsibilities ($K)	5000	GLC program cost ($K):		20
Loss on revenues (%):	5	GLC program duration (hrs):		35
		Opportunity cost to company (%):		60
Impact Cost (Revenues):	**$250,000**	**GLC Program Total Cost:**	**$49,167**	

Sunk Cost ($):	**$818,281**	**Replacement Cost:**	**$1,156,000**
Burn Rate ($/Mo)	**$69,010**	**Payback (Mo):**	**0.7**

Howard

Howard hated politics. He couldn't distinguish between politics which he considered sleazy and understanding the politics in his department or company. He was a project manager who had to supervise six people whom he could not inspire. He had to work with ten peers in order to continue with the challenging technical assignment.

Howard, Project Manager, was unapproachable. He seemed too distracted for others to bring him a new problem. Howard's office was cluttered with projects. His mind was cluttered, too. He spoke like a broken computer in fits and spurts of information so jammed with facts that people walked away shaking their heads. He was supposed to be the business team leader of a project in a defense company which was trying to become a commercial company.

Howard was affable and polite. His voice was soft and his demeanor was quite immature. He spoke, though, from such an intellectual perspective that nobody wanted to be in a meeting with him. He was supposed to be the team leader, yet he could not communicate with his subordinates or colleagues. The ten peers he was to interact with would end up shaking their heads after meetings, and re-do his work and their work to try to make some cohesive sense of projects in which they were mutually involved. His subordinates never knew exactly what he wanted so they ran off in directions which were eventually red-lined by Howard.

Howard finally got the message. Actually, he had been quite unhappy, knowing he was flunking as a manager and he wanted to stay involved with the interesting project.

When Howard was convinced that his impact on others was confusing, he set about with a tool kit of disciplinary maneuvers. We asked him to pre-think each meeting and draw an outline of concrete goals expected from every discussion. He was to discipline himself not to go off on a tangent. In the first meeting, the colleagues were dumbfounded. Of course, they were sure it wouldn't last, but eventually, all the previously absent players started appearing at meetings.

Can you imagine the Red Ink that had been splattered about by Howard's meandering and lack of strategic direction? Without any understanding of the politics of an organization, Howard could never strategize about who had the power and how to go about getting decisions made. He quickly learned, and began to enjoy thinking through the strategy for getting things done in an efficient manner. He even started thinking from his peer's perspective about things.

The cost of disgruntled employees who sabotaged Howard's projects had been very expensive. When all of this was calculated, Howard was asked to give up as business leader.

You might wonder, now, about how Howard's demotion could be a successful answer. The transformation of Howard was a journey. He had some soul-searching to do. Although he learned how to be more political, he still decided that he did not want the headaches of managing others.

He had hated the management tasks of his job, and when he began to sound more succinct, he began to obtain more support for his ideas. Now he is senior scientist and a technical guru at each meeting. Should he go into management again, he knows what to do. In the meantime, he is practicing speaking in outlines. He does not allow himself to ramble.

Howard also changed his speech patterns which created a dramatic effect. He spoke louder and more forcefully and he learned to **underline** some words and put exclamation marks at the end of some sentences!

Instead of having to leave the company, Howard is a productive and influential team member who actually learned to communicate at many new levels. He is no longer a financial handicap and, additionally, he feels satisfied and energetic about his work.

Costimator for Howard:

GLC Red Ink Behavior   -   Costimator Analysis

Please supply the following information:		ID:	50

* Include all benefits in salaries (e.g., stocks, bonuses, insurances, etc...)

Last:		First: Howard	Company	LMF Corp
Title:	Proj Mgr			
Problem Description:	Not political (non-mgr type)			

Salary ($K/yr)*:	100	Severance package ($K):	100
DEP's lost hours/week:	2	Search hiring ($K):	30
Problem duration (Mo):	12	Training ($K):	20
Direct Cost:	**$5,000**	**Replacement Cost:**	**$150,000**

Manager's sal ($K/yr)*:	200	HR person's sal ($K/yr)*:	60
Manager's lost hrs/wk:	3	HR person's lost hrs/wk:	1
Dur. of intervention (Mo):	3	Other persons ($K/wk):	0
	Intervention Cost:	**$4,125**	

Number of peers:	10	Number of subordinates:	6
Peers' salary ($K/yr)*:	100	Subordinates' salary ($K/yr)*:	68
Peers' lost hrs/wk:	5	Subordinates' lost hrs/wk:	6
	Impact Cost (People):	**$186,200**	

Revenues responsibilities ($K)	500	GLC program cost ($K):	9
Loss on revenues (%):	2	GLC program duration (hrs):	15
		Opportunity cost to company (%):	25
Impact Cost (Revenues):	**$10,000**	**GLC Program Total Cost:**	**$9,977**

Sunk Cost ($):	**$205,325**	**Replacement Cost:**	**$150,000**
Burn Rate ($/Mo)	**$18,142**	**Payback (Mo):**	**0.5**

Ted

Ted, Vice President of Marketing, in a high tech corporation, was tiring everyone in his path. Ted, the answer man, was compulsive about having the right answer. His boss, peers or subordinates did not know this. They just believed Ted was a cumbersome, bothersome pain in the neck about details. They discounted his calls for help and they ignored his lengthy memos because he seemed to be so obsessive about some parts of the big puzzle.

Ted was sent to our company to learn strategic thinking and planning. He was so bent on the tactics of the position that he was perceived as a small thinking executive who could never hold the title of business team Vice President. Oh, he was vice president all right, but he appeared to be doing the job of a tech support person. He wasted the time of eleven peers and seven subordinates. He was in charge of one of the largest financial projects in his company. His CCO and CEO were disappointed in him and he was feeling ignored when major shifts or crises occurred.

With an exploration of Ted's belief system, we discovered his fundamental supposition was that to be effective he should have the answers to all of the major questions in his dominion. This meant that when the CEO asked anything about circuit boards or fabrication issues within his enormous product area, he thought he needed to have the answer at his fingertips.

This belief system started with a strong set of consequences from his lawyer-father who insisted that his kids answered every one of his questions. Even in college, Ted believed every question deserved an answer. Of course, he was highly rewarded when he did have the answers!

In his billion dollar company, Ted was not expected to have every answer at his fingertips. But, his search for every answer was difficult to give up. He liked sounding prepared and he enjoyed showing off among his eleven peers.

The fight for data, however, was ponderous and circuitous and no one understood his compulsive quest. It took days in our office to convince Ted that his search was not paying off. He had to perceive that he was seen as ridiculous and a "dinosaur brain" to continue to seek all answers. The "dinosaur brain" label hurts and we use it whenever we can. It means you revert back to a primitive response when you are anxious. The primal response is not sophisticated. It is a reflex born from centuries when we used fight or flight as our only coping response.

Ted's homework drills were just as simple as many of our assignments. This work can appear primal. Sometimes it is so slippery and elusive that we don't know what we don't know about ourselves. We often miss those blind spots because the other side of the behavior is what makes us successful. Because we don't want to give up the positive piece of the behavior, when it is threatened, the first instinct is to defend the behavior.

Ted was asked to say, "I don't know" as often as he possibly could. We asked him to count the times he said this, reporting to us the hopefully growing number each week. In the beginning, Ted just took a leap of faith with us. He was terrified to admit there was something he did not know. He was actually quite amazed that no one seemed to even notice or care! The positive response to Ted was about his relaxed style. Colleagues did not have to guard themselves around Ted, and they like it. This was a baffling result for Ted. "You

mean, all they want me to be is relaxed. What about content?"
he screamed.

Ted was doing all or nothing thinking again. He ultimately
came to learn that when the delivery didn't sound like a court
room, and people were no longer worried that Ted would want
to catch them not doing their homework, they would become
interested in the content of what Ted had to say. The second-
ary gain was that Ted could be puzzled and unsure of himself
some of the time, and nobody seemed to mind. The irony is
that they seemed to like it!

The second part of the assignment was to point the questioner
in the direction of one of Ted's subordinates or peers. He was
to count his hand-offs, increasing them weekly. In the beginning Ted was wary about what he would do with his time.

Amazingly, Ted now had time for strategic thinking. He
delighted his boss with a situational analysis of his product
line. He designed an observance and planning procedure to
make major policy decisions in his area of responsibility. The
CEO complimented Ted within a week, and soon he was
invited to business team strategic meetings.

It took Ted a while to incorporate the notion of **strategic** with
every move he made. We quoted SGI's Ken Coleman who
lectures to his company with the story that many people ask
him for more strategic jobs and he counters with the idea that
every job is strategic—if you will just look at it from that
perspective!

Ted doesn't worry about being right anymore. He knows that
he needs to prioritize his quests for data and he does that on a
daily basis. We remind him of another favorite person of
GLC, Ed Zchau, who was President of a company and a

California congressman and even a Vice Presidential nominee. Ed is very comfortable with saying "I don't know". This can put people at ease, and we never believe he is stupid or lazy.

We believe, and Ted now does too, that the brilliant and strategic thinkers prioritize the answers they want to acquire, leaving trivia to others, data for appropriate colleagues, and a willingness to research when necessary. Ted puts his feet up on the desk now, looks out the windows and dreams the possible new strategies for his department, happily!

Costimator for Ted:

GLC Red Ink Behavior   -   Costimator Analysis

Please supply the following information:		ID: 51

* Include all benefits in salaries (e.g., stocks, bonuses, insurances, etc...)

Last:		First: Ted		Company	ABC
Title:	VP				
Problem Description:	Arrogant				

Salary ($K/yr)*:	175	Severance package ($K):	175	
DEP's lost hours/week:	4	Search hiring ($K):	55	
Problem duration (Mo):	12	Training ($K):	15	
Direct Cost:	**$17,500**	**Replacement Cost:**	**$245,000**	

Manager's sal ($K/yr)*:	250	HR person's sal ($K/yr)*:	50
Manager's lost hrs/wk:	2	HR person's lost hrs/wk:	1
Dur.of intervention (Mo):	3	Other persons ($K/wk):	0
Intervention Cost:		**$3,437**	

Number of peers:	11	Number of subordinates:	7
Peers' salary ($K/yr)*:	160	Subordinates' salary ($K/yr)*:	125
Peers' lost hrs/wk:	2	Subordinates' lost hrs/wk:	3
Impact Cost (People):		**$153,625**	

Revenues responsibilities ($K)	0	GLC program cost ($K):	15
Loss on revenues (%):	0	GLC program duration (hrs):	30
		Opportunity cost to company (%):	30
Impact Cost (Revenues):	**$0**	**GLC Program Total Cost:**	**$18,555**

Sunk Cost ($):	**$174,563**	**Replacement Cost:**	**$245,000**
Burn Rate ($/Mo)	**$15,406**	**Payback (Mo):**	**1.2**

Teresa

Teresa, a talented and brilliant mid-level manager, was supervising three reports and interacted with seven peers. When the company did a corporation-wide 360, her scores indicated that others at all levels thought Teresa was abusive, dominating and demonstrated bulldozer behavior. Her manager simply wanted her to show more empathy for others. Since her position was in a people-related field, her manager believed she should model a nurturing stance. She, however, held a significant position which covered many serious and technical areas for which one significant slip could affect hundreds of people and the company's reputation at large.

Teresa was single, young, energetic and opinionated. Her peers tried to avoid her and missed meetings and data to escape her tirades. Her three subordinates used sick leave days and begged for extra-curricular work to recuperate from her outbursts. They claimed they could not think straight when she stood over them. She had the highest turn-over rate in her department, and she was always below her head count allowances.

Teresa lost about two hours a week of her own productive time because she would either be fuming mad over poor product quality or feeling misunderstood and sad because no one seemed to want to cooperate with her, no less go out to lunch with her. She had no friends on the job and, thus, spent hours trying to justify her outbursts.

Teresa did not appreciate our feedback, nor did she appreciate the opportunity to use our coaching program as an avenue for insight, change and promotion. Instead she saw us as punishment and she attended the first several sessions with arms folded and receptivity also folded.

At one point our coach simulated what he would feel like should he have receive such damaging feedback. Another coach made a whimpering sound and this touched off the vulnerability in Teresa. She cried, asked for forgiveness for crying, and cried some more. We called this a breakthrough and told her so. She had no capacity for comforting herself and asked to be excused for the day.

Before we helped her to go, we asked her to name two empty chairs in the room. One was the nurturing chair and one was the critical chair. We then asked her to speak her feelings between the two chairs. She could only muster up that she was very tired.

Then we asked Teresa to listen for a response from one of the chairs. Of course, the critical chair spoke right up, admonishing Teresa for being so pathetic. We asked Teresa to go sit in that chair and finish the tirade. She was very articulate, including, "If you hadn't stayed up so late last night you would not have been so fragile today."

When we insisted Teresa sit in the nurturing chair, she was silent. She did not know how to talk in a comforting way to herself, much less to her subordinates! For the next several sessions we insisted that Teresa practice self-comforting. This is an exercise we use with seventy-five percent of our leadership candidates. Men and women alike seem unable to soothe themselves. Their standards for excellence are so high that they are continually disappointing themselves. Few of us are strong enough to do everything perfectly. The higher the bar, the fewer the self-congratulating thoughts or actions, the more anxiety expressed in the face of stress.

By the way, we don't always use two or more coaches per session, but Teresa's dominating presence required this in the early stages.

Eventually, Teresa discovered how good it felt to be kind to herself. We often said the words for her. Much of our work is giving clients words to try on. At first employees feel silly and refuse this indulgence. Since we guarantee that emotional soothing is a concomitant to maturity, and we sell that concept with great vigor, candidates usually try to do it. One CFO woman actually asked for a list of feelings which accompanied faces to match the feelings. She began to get in touch with her feelings in this way. She would say something or explain something and we would ask her to look at the chart and identify a feeling.

Teresa learned to recognize her own emotional responses and then she raised her own consciousness to be alert to feelings in others. When she realized that feelings do not have to make sense, she relaxed and even allowed her subordinates to have irrelevant responses some of the time.

Now that Teresa could recognize her own feelings, her drill was to spot some in others, take a guess about what might be going on for them, and state those feelings for her colleagues. "I'll bet you're feeling a little frightened right now because I usually come down pretty hard on you when I discover this kind of an error. You might really be anxious about meeting with me."

The response to Teresa was immediate and encouraging. The more that people talked to each other and eventually to her boss, the more relaxed Teresa began to feel. She was amazed at how easy it was, and how much more productive the team seemed to be because she took one or two minutes to do some reflecting back.

The last and hardest assignment for Teresa was to regularly show her own vulnerability to her staff. In the beginning she refused to do this assignment and she balked over several other attempts to help her to express herself even to us. We wore her down. The way we wore her down was to have her come into our office when she was beat up, beat down, anxious, tired, deflated and lonely.

For a beautiful and bright woman, Teresa had no social life. The job was her life. When we could just be nurturing for her and she believed we understood and were not just patronizing her, she eagerly came in to vent her distress. Noticing how good this felt, she decided she could give the same thing to others. But, to unburden herself was too much. She was a private person. We have heard that statement in our office hundreds of times! To which we always answer: "We know you are a private person. We do not want you to become so vulnerable that you are rendered powerless. We just want you to let out a little steam so that you have some logic left to deal with the concrete problems of your position."

So, eventually Teresa told us her stories, her birthday aloneness, her solo lunches at her desk, her envy over the happy laughter in the hall, the men who went hunting together and the women and men who went out for drinks or coffee occasionally.

Eventually, Teresa shared these lonely feelings with her administrative assistant, one of her peers, and one of her subordinates. And eventually, she shared her disappointment over her 360 review with her boss. And eventually, Teresa became real to her colleagues. They still understood her standards, but they were more relaxed around her, and when the next birthday came around, guess what? Teresa threw herself a party and every one in the department came. She brought the roses in the next day to show us.

Costimator for Teresa:

GLC Red Ink Behavior - Costimator Analysis

Please supply the following information:	ID:	52

* Include all benefits in salaries (e.g., stocks, bonuses, insurances, etc...)

Last:		First:	Teresa	Company	PQR
Title:	Mgr				
Problem Description:	Intimidating				

Salary ($K/yr)*:	75	Severance package ($K):	75
DEP's lost hours/week:	2	Search hiring ($K):	35
Problem duration (Mo):	12	Training ($K):	12
Direct Cost:	**$3,750**	**Replacement Cost:**	**$122,000**

Manager's sal ($K/yr)*:	100	HR person's sal ($K/yr)*:	45
Manager's lost hrs/wk:	1	HR person's lost hrs/wk:	3
Dur.of intervention (Mo):	3	Other persons ($K/wk):	0
	Intervention Cost:	**$1,469**	

Number of peers:	7	Number of subordinates:	3
Peers' salary ($K/yr)*:	75	Subordinates' salary ($K/yr)*:	60
Peers' lost hrs/wk:	4	Subordinates' lost hrs/wk:	6
	Impact Cost (People):	**$79,500**	

Revenues responsibilities ($K)	0	GLC program cost ($K):	9
Loss on revenues (%):	0	GLC program duration (hrs):	12
		Opportunity cost to company (%):	25
Impact Cost (Revenues):	**$0**	**GLC Program Total Cost:**	**$9,586**

Sunk Cost ($):	**$84,719**	**Replacement Cost:**	**$122,000**
Burn Rate ($/Mo)	**$7,427**	**Payback (Mo):**	**1.3**

Hank

Hank, Director, Manufacturing, was a $300,000 a year man who had six direct reports and four peers who interacted with him on a daily basis.

Hank had lost most of his group and most of his tasks. As a 20 year veteran with the computer company, Hank was not terminated, just derailed. His position shrank from Director level to an individual contributor who was not contributing. Hank had some rebuilding to do. He was as technically brilliant as ever. He had just stopped collaborating three years ago. Why?

Our first task was to understand the cluster of events which sent Hank spiraling down. The problem was personal, a child in his family accused Hank of something dreadful, although Hank was finally acquitted of charges. He made a judgment error with a major customer of the company. His wife sued for divorce. He gained a great deal of weight. He lost his secretary of 15 years. The VP who had hired him, sponsored him, and yes, enabled him, retired. Hank was without resources and too worn out to seek help.

Fortunately, an alert HR person directed Hank to us. Our first task was to attend an off-site retreat in which we got to see the sullen, mean-spirited Hank in full motion. He was abrupt, distanced himself from small talk, and seemed to point out logic flaws to others with great zeal.

In our early sessions we urged Hank to take the leap of faith that he could rebuild his reputation with the team around him. This took a series of meetings in which Hank was to repair relationships with each person. The list was very long. We taught Hank reflective listening and he started each meeting with: "I think I've been a miserable chap in the last years and I want to repair our relationship. Can you tell me how to begin this with you?"

Some of his "enemies" were actually helpful, some had given up on Hank and would not give him information, and some simply avoided the confrontation by claiming that there had never been a problem. Hank was fully prepared for each type of answer. He learned to ask multiple choice questions like: "Are you still upset about Comdex '94, or do you want to talk about my dressing you down in public last November in front of the IOC guys?"

Some of the conflicts were deep and personal and took many meetings to unravel. Some of the colleagues simply accepted that Hank had gone through a series of bad times and that he was acting under duress. Several actually shared their own tribulations and Hank became the father confessor or the good listening ear. He was amazed at what people were willing to share. He ended up with three good friends with whom he still plays golf.

The next step was to ask for sponsorship from these people for new responsibilities. Some did not trust the new Hank, and he spoke the concerns out loud for them. He showed them ways they could monitor their trust level and Hank needed to continually persuade them that this was important to him. Cranky Hanky was slipping away.

It was not long before Hank was beginning to trust himself again. Instead of the retirement he had been planning, he took on a two year plum assignment, which was offered, much to his surprise, just six months after our coaching began. Hank was careful about the level of supervision and collaboration required of this new assignment. He finally declared, however, that all positions require some understanding of the politics of the organization. The company was happy to use him in some new productive ways. The financial drain had been plugged. And Hank was rejuvenated.

Costimator for Hank:

GLC Red Ink Behavior - Costimator Analysis

Please supply the following information: ID: 53

* Include all benefits in salaries (e.g., stocks, bonuses, insurances, etc...)

| Last: | | First: Hank | | Company | DEF |

Title: Dr

Problem Description: Non collaborative

Salary ($K/yr)*:	300	Severance package ($K):	250
DEP's lost hours/week:	2	Search hiring ($K):	100
Problem duration (Mo):	12	Training ($K):	18

| Direct Cost: | $15,000 | | Replacement Cost: | $368,000 |

Manager's sal ($K/yr)*:	500	HR person's sal ($K/yr)*:	100
Manager's lost hrs/wk:	1	HR person's lost hrs/wk:	3
Dur.of intervention (Mo):	3	Other persons ($K/wk):	0

| Intervention Cost: | | $5,000 |

Number of peers:	4	Number of subordinates:	6
Peers' salary ($K/yr)*:	300	Subordinates' salary ($K/yr)*:	215
Peers' lost hrs/wk:	3	Subordinates' lost hrs/wk:	4

| Impact Cost (People): | | $219,000 |

Revenues responsibilities ($K)	150	GLC program cost ($K):	18
Loss on revenues (%):	10	GLC program duration (hrs):	30
		Opportunity cost to company (%):	50

| Impact Cost (Revenues): | $15,000 | GLC Program Total Cost: | $25,031 |

Sunk Cost ($):	$254,000	Replacement Cost:	$368,000
Burn Rate ($/Mo)	$22,417	Payback (Mo):	1.1

Martha

Martha was great with her team, her subordinates loved her, and her peers thought she was a collaborating darling. Her two-in-a-box bosses thought she was a hellion. She missed their meetings, spoke up rebelliously in their meetings, and bad-mouthed them in her own staff meetings at every turn. Martha had not learned to manage up.

Martha was Director of Marketing and responsible for seven support people and interacted with two colleagues whose work overlapped with hers. Her two in a box bosses were the cause of red ink flow in this case.

Rebellion is expensive. Because her two bosses had a great deal of responsibility which she seemed to discard and prioritize at the bottom of her list, Martha was a financial and personal liability to Bob and Raj. After we researched her background to discover an excessively disciplinarian father and a mother who provided an environment for rebellion, and a history of school and college disturbances, Martha recognized her pattern. Getting in trouble with the authority figure made her quite popular with her peers. That had worked for many years.

When we pointed out that anti-authoritarianism called for a big price tag, we wondered together if she were weary of being on strike with her bosses, wherever they were. Martha declared that she wanted to get in line but she despised both men. Later we learned that she set a higher standard for men and for her bosses than for everyone else. "They shouldn't be incompetent in anything," she shouted. Patterns of disappointment in her teachers, her gym coach and her first bosses spilled out.

When a test for anti-authoritarianism pushed her way off the charts, Martha decided it was time to grow up. This meant establishing a give-and-take relationship with both Bob and Raj. This also meant seeing their idiosyncrasies and allowing for their individual differences. She had to work harder to anticipate their needs. She resented this feverishly at first, but eventually realized that her subordinates certainly have to figure her out sometimes.

She realized that she was much easier on everyone than she was on Bob and Raj. When the notion of making them successful was introduced, Martha laughed. Since they were mature gentlemen, we met together in conflict resolution sessions in our office. They did this for Martha.

Martha began to see the way she set them up. She also learned how inadequate they both felt in being unable to motivate her to see their priorities. She was surprised at their candid declarations to her and they won her over when they asked directly for her support of their goals. A touching meeting ensued when Martha explained her long-term rebellion and asked for their cooperation in helping her recognize when she was undermining their directives.

The bonus for Martha was that she gained new respect from her peers who were always perplexed by her insubordination. Her own subordinates also reinforced her changes because they too wanted success for Bob and Raj. They had always felt in the middle. Now they felt she represented their interests and the bosses fairly.

The cost of Martha to the company was relatively lower because she was not hard on her own direct reports. The escalation of costs comes when each difficult moment exponentially rains down on a subordinate, and, then, often onto their subordinates. The trickle down did not occur in Martha's case. The cost, however, of a highly priced boss's time is certainly a factor in her red ink analysis.

Martha has a lot more time now that she doesn't have to make the boss wrong. She even campaigned for Raj to the president the other day. She was proud of herself and the president congratulated her on being such a loyal constituent. As long as Martha knows she has the right to point out flagrant problems and that she has an obligation to present solutions to those problems along with the complaint, Martha is riding rapidly to the top of her own lofty goals.

Costimator for Martha:

GLC Red Ink Behavior - Costimator Analysis

Please supply the following information:	ID:	54

* Include all benefits in salaries (e.g., stocks, bonuses, insurances, etc...)

Last:		First:	Martha	Company	HIJ

Title:	Dr. Mktg
Problem Description:	Couldn't manage up. Rebellious

Salary ($K/yr)*:	150	Severance package ($K):	150
DEP's lost hours/week:	3	Search hiring ($K):	50
Problem duration (Mo):	12	Training ($K):	22
Direct Cost:	**$11,250**	**Replacement Cost:**	**$222,000**

Manager's sal ($K/yr)*:	400	HR person's sal ($K/yr)*:	75
Manager's lost hrs/wk:	6	HR person's lost hrs/wk:	1
Dur.of intervention (Mo):	3	Other persons ($K/wk):	0
	Intervention Cost:	**$15,469**	

Number of peers:	2	Number of subordinates:	7
Peers' salary ($K/yr)*:	150	Subordinates' salary ($K/yr)*:	80
Peers' lost hrs/wk:	1	Subordinates' lost hrs/wk:	0.25
	Impact Cost (People):	**$11,000**	

Revenues responsibilities ($K)	500	GLC program cost ($K):	12
Loss on revenues (%):	5	GLC program duration (hrs):	25
		Opportunity cost to company (%):	25
Impact Cost (Revenues):	**$25,000**	**GLC Program Total Cost:**	**$14,441**

Sunk Cost ($):	**$62,719**	**Replacement Cost:**	**$222,000**
Burn Rate ($/Mo)	**$9,094**	**Payback (Mo):**	**1.6**

What Other Deadly Behaviors Drain a Company?

We have cited some fairly simple cases of interpersonal attributes that needed tuning up. Most of the cases sound like those above. Another set of ingredients which drain resources are behaviors which encompass procrastination, lack of organization, presentation skills, time management and political naiveté. Those areas are easy to work on when the belief systems and sacred cows about perfectionism and self-confidence are restored.

Other areas we assist with are negotiation and persuasion skill-building. We help folks sell themselves and other worthy causes. All of the leadership qualities of delegation, giving and taking critical feedback and managing up seem to fall in place when the self-esteem and the self-awareness of a client's impact on others is handled.

Dysfunctional behaviors occur in radio stations, plumbing companies, newspapers, chambers of commerce, and any setting in which the working styles of one person impact the working styles of another.

When an executive with a problem behavior contemplates change, he is often fearful and overwhelmed with the worry of completely overhauling a behavior or himself.

The 3% Rule of Change!

When you deliver the news that your employee or colleague needs a major working style overhaul, he can become para-lyzed sullen, demoralized or just plain overwhelmed. You may also be overwhelmed about coaching that kind of a shift. You may worry that the change in an employee's behavior might be asking for too much. If you use the rule of 3% minimum change, no one will be frustrated or discouraged.

Will the difficult employee have to change all of his spots? No. After all, he is a great financial person, or she is your best sales person, but there are some changes the company has decided are necessary.

You are not asking anyone to change his or her basic personality. You are simply asking them to add some enhancements to existing behaviors or subtract a set of habits which no longer work for their new stature in the organization. New managers need to learn to delegate, to make more strategic decisions or to show more charisma in meetings. Some of those shifts are very intimidating.

There are some changes which require immediate movement. In these cases, critical changes need drastic responses. The situation can't wait for just 3% increments. "You may never raise your hand in anger in this company again!" may be very good coaching.

Crisis coaching is quite different from development coaching. In development coaching you are talking about overhauling the major working style in order to reduce micro-management, help the client develop a powerful style, or help them to be a strategic thinker. These are not small tasks, and they are major shifts, but they are not life-threatening even though, eventually, they can be career- threatening.

We came upon the 3% rule quite by accident. An engineer who had worked for a blue chip computer company was unhappy with his progress on the company tennis ladder. He would go into each game thinking he had to do 100% better than he'd done on the last game. Of course, the anxiety and high expectations he had for himself would ruin his game. Even when he thought he should play only 50% better, he seemed to worry himself into a poorer game.

So, our friend decided to write a computer program to analyze exactly how many points better he should have for each game in order to improve his status on the ladder. It became so interesting that he took the entire 400 players and devised a system for analyzing what percentage per game they would each need to improve in order to move up the ladder in the next season. The results were amazing. Not 50%, not 25%, not 10%!

He learned that a trifling 3% improvement in each game would catapult him and every other employee into the next tier. How easy 3% seemed. Without the tension and high expectations for himself, he actually made a 42% improvement in one season.

The point is you don't have to do it all the first round or in the first game.. Lowering expectations for your employees gives rise to the pleasant opportunity to create immediate improvement. The paradox is that lowering the bar will motivate rather than discourage change.

At GLC we like to see people stretch and we believe that *the sky's the limit*! However, when we are asking executives to make major shifts in the way they approach their business lives, the 3% challenge is easier for beginning the process.

Changes need positive reinforcement. If you are the agent of change, don't forget that reinforcement will encourage and ultimately cement the change. If you see a 3% improvement, talk about it! The all or nothing supervisor doesn't expect to do this. He will comment on the final product only. Except that the final product may be very slow to arrive.

Successful supervisors and mentors set ambitious goals but they urge and monitor and acknowledge small improvements. Each smile or accolade builds courage for the next move. You can compliment with: "Hey, the effort was there. You didn't get the result, but now you have some practice in negotiating, or giving honest feedback."

The last reason why small increments work is because the colleagues around your employee will notice behavioral differences and comment on these small changes. Usually the moves are much larger than the 3%, and, so, of course, others notice. But participants in our programs, and your colleagues around you, only need to think about the first small steps in showing more humor, giving up sarcasm, not blaming others, showing compassion, or giving up territorialism.

Try your own three percent change. You can't lose the whole fifty pounds today. You can't turn into an extrovert tomorrow. And you can't become the perfect manager yet. Give yourself a few more days...

Chapter Six

Now What?

Congratulations! You have done your homework and you are ready to refer that difficult employee. You may even have decided to address your own working style habits or idiosyncracies. The human resource people in your organization are trained to look at and handle difficult situations and employees. We believe that they should be your first stop.

If you are the Human Resource person in your organization, we know that sometimes you have a very hard sell to make to the manager of your identified problem person. Sometimes his manager is really the problem. We hope the costimator will be a starting point. Now you can at least talk about what the messy employee is costing.

If you don't feel you've been heard, or the action suggested by a consultant does not seem to fit your style or your case, ask

again. Try another professional within your company. Ask a
manager who seems to be handling the likes of a *red-inker* very
well. Each year human resource departments become more
sophisticated and more open to your involvement than any time
in the history of employee relations.

When To Consider Outsourcing

So, when should your company outsource the function of
assisting an employee who is causing problems in the company? Or, when should you spend money to enhance the skills
of a potential star? Many times, employee problems can be
well handled by your in-house specialists such as the employee
relations people in Human Resources. The main reasons for
outsourcing are the concern for employee confidentiality or the
issue of trust in the company which some employees seem to
lose. Other employee problems are just so cumbersome or
long term that they are not worth the organization's internal
resources.

When an employee has had a long-standing problem with no
visible improvement, along with many sessions with in-house
people, outsourcing should be considered. The cost of chronic
problem employees mounts up over time. Something that
could have been stopped by an aggressive timely intervention
can drag on and on, literally dragging everyone else involved
down as well.

Another case where outsourcing makes sense is with high level
employees where there is no peer who has the knowledge and
capability of creating change. Until the last two years, highest
level executives were excluded from the general 360 testing.
Now, they too can get feedback about themselves. All too

often, the problem is ignored or hidden, or the people around this person are afraid to tell the truth anyway.

An employee with trust issues to begin with will often worry about internal departments making suggestions to him. If someone from outside the company is the mediator, a lot of the pressure in the conflict situation is relieved. The company can remain objective, allowing the consulting company to take the "heavy" role. The "at risk" employee is much more likely to trust the firm chosen to do an intervention than they are to trust anyone from within the company. Part of the reason for this is that almost everyone in the company has an agenda while the facilitating outsource company only has one: To resolve the problem effectively and quickly.

This all sounds quite self-serving. Let me announce, then, that there are many things that we cannot do. The real leverage for change comes from inside, from the boss or respected person who can influence the employee's future in the company. An outside resource is sometimes thought of as being more objective. Unfortunately, this is not always so. People and behavioral management is not an exact science. Sensitive issues can be taken care of outside normal company channels, but we do believe the company's involvement in the problem enhances success potential.

One important factor in the entire process of employee change needs to be understood from the very beginning. The referring party must be committed to the change. Backing down or hesitating will only postpone the work in the long run. Leverage from the company that the change is mandatory enhances the process.

The most critical success factor is the motivational level of the employee. He or she often needs to be motivated by serious consequences in order to make the change long term and permanent. If there is not complete top-down support on this intervention, the project's success is compromised.

The Hesitation Steps. We remind managers and human resource executives about this step. It is the moment, or weeks, between deciding to do something about this difficult person, and the precise instant when you have to confront him. We hesitate because we become unsure. Are we doing the right thing? Do we have the right to judge?

The second area of hesitation occurs when we anticipate the reaction by the identified employee. Will he quit, scream, kill himself (that has been a consideration) or just hate you for the rest of your life? Sometimes the expectations around the response put the intervention off for years. Later the employee rants, "why didn't someone ever have the courage to tell me?"

The other end of the hesitation comes when you have given the news and the employee turns the whole problem back on to you. This can become crazy-making. Remember, you are not the problem. He is an expert in making others wrong, and defending himself from the reality. Plan on a tense meeting. Nobody likes to be told they are a problem. The more difficult the employee, of course, the more difficult the response will be.

When choosing an outsource company, look for certain qualities in the program which can help to insure results. All too often development companies spend the major time on assessment of the employee, delivering reams of material on his attributes and liabilities, with little time left for the difficult part of coaching change with tools and drills to shift old habits to new ways of doing business. Be sure that the actual intervention is short term but that the outsource company guarantees long term results. The new employee behavior needs to become a habit and the outsource company needs to know how to create these kinds of outcomes.

How to Manage the Outsource Company

It's important to have excellent communication between the problem employee's company and the outsource company so that changes can be monitored internally. It's essential that the employing company have a clear idea of what kinds of results are desired. Specific changes should be listed and agreed on with the outsource company in advance. This list of changes will be communicated to the employee. You must set deadlines for results along with intermediate checkpoints and review these regularly.

Expect hiccups. Employees sometimes get so terrified of being appraised that they go to desperate means to distract away from themselves. They will try to cause a rift between your interventionist and their boss. They may lie. They may hope to divide and conquer with double messages to and from the intervention group. We experience this on a daily basis. Being prepared for difficult reactions and keeping your own ego intact helps.

Your outsource company can help the employee get an experience of change by practicing new behaviors rather than giving only lecture classes or batteries of assessment evaluations which may not actually create change but only educate the employee.

Education is important, but actual change comes about through consciousness-raising and regular practice. The internal experiential change sinks in to a place no theory has ever been able to penetrate. It is much like driver's education. You can read manuals about driving, but practicing with all the multi-tasking of head, feet and hand movements, as well as being aware of the environment, actually requires experiencing being behind the wheel.

Many of our referred employees have MBAs, have read the latest motivational books and can quote from the *Seven Habits* and many of Tom Peters' good words. Intellectually, they are aware, but emotionally they may not be able to see or hear what they are doing to themselves and others.

The process of employee coaching involves the following steps which we use in all of our programs.

1.   Alert the employee about his or her problems. Create awareness in the individual employee that he or she may have a problem behavior and that this working style or habit is hampering his chance for success. Show him how this is happening so that he can start to become more objective about his behavior

2.   Help the employee understand and equate his behavioral impact on others, boss, peers, subordinates and, of course, on himself. Leverage is built when the employee knows that the feedback is not one isolated case.

3.   Teach the skills to create the change in behavior. With homework and drills, the employee will practice being different in situations which call for varying behaviors.

4.   Advertise changes.   Announce the possibility of new behavior so others will be alert to his changes. Others have been programmed to expect certain behavior from him. It often takes a campaign for colleagues to really take note of positive changes. Without this, the candidate has no chance for positive reinforcement.

5.   Set up a continuous feedback loop. Ask for sponsors or agents of your change This feedback will strengthen change potential.

6.   Create a maintenance program. Continue classes or coaching in some arena which will enhance the first era of the changes. Since gathering awareness requires the longest period of growth, many people actually change very little in the first intervention. They eventually make dramatic changes, of course, which are seen and produce results. They feel better about their working styles and they really get attention.

Choosing a company to work with on the challenging topics described in this book can be rather a daunting task. You must have confidence that the outsource company can do the job. In the meantime, how they do the job may seem a bit mysterious. It's important to make sure they can describe exactly what the process is and how it works.

You should expect that the company you decide to work with can tell you precisely what is involved in changing a problem employee into an outstanding contributor. Once you've narrowed the choices down, a good way to determine which company will suit your needs is to "test" the best candidate by sending an employee to go through an initial program. If the

process the outsource company uses is successful in this one
instance, more than likely other employees will benefit as well.

Items to Look for in Choosing the Outsourcing Company:

Expect the company to:

1. Give you details of how they work with your employees and what the process of change involves.
2. Hold staff consultations about your employee.
3. Suggest reliable and valid working style and personality tests to augment feedback from the company.
4. Use some form of 360 feedback tests for colleagues.
5. Invite champions and nemeses of employee to meetings.
6. Videotape to highlight blind spots.
7. Observe employee in meetings on site.
8. Meet regularly with referring HR and referring manager.
9. Maintain confidentiality, urging ombudsman qualities as the employee begins to trust his coach.
10. Offer list of satisfied clients as references.
11. Guarantee that you will get the results or the organization will continue to work until goals are delivered.
12. Be confident in their approach to your individual situation.
13. Explain the failures as well as the successes.
14. Sound more innovative and provocative and objective than your in-house staff members are permitted to be.
15. Be courageous in confronting employees and management.
16. Love their work.

How to Sleep Nights

Good people worry about their employees, colleagues and superiors. They want everyone to be successful. You may even be one of those good people. In order not to stay awake nights worrying over your part in this employees dilemma, we suggest the following ideas.

Tell the truth. *Red ink behaviors* hurt everyone. Whenever you are talking to or about a difficult employee, tell your truth. If you have to stutter around and feel awkward with the feedback, say so. Start with, "This is really tough for me. I don't know how to start this, and I am worrying about your reaction already. But I want you to know that....."

Plan on a reaction. Whenever we have feedback that hurts, we are going to react. Some employees will implode, hold all feelings inside and you may just see a frozen or polite face. Be wary of this. You can even help a little with, "If I were receiving what I just talked about, I'd be feeling pretty bad right now. Is this hard for you to take?"

Plan on a big reaction. When the less stoic types have a reaction to your complaint, feedback or suggestion, plan on a strong reaction. His first response may be to blame. He will blame the messenger or others around the problem. He may call you out of line, and incriminate every situation and everyone involved. Allow for this blaming reaction. It is only phase one of the response.

Plan on noise. There may be shouting. There may be sniffling. There may be the sound of a slamming door. This is still phase one. Try to be comfortable with the response. No one enjoys critical feedback about himself. If you believe the responder has not sufficiently vented, respond with the three magic words: Not, *I love you*. Respond with the three fool-proof communication enhancers: *Tell me more!*

He will become the attorney. He will ask you to defend your accusations. The more rational the employee, the more details he will want. The legalistic employee is usually very good at deflecting blame because he is used to defending himself. He is often a master at denial and even better at putting others on the defensive. He is used to winning. He may ask you to name names, give examples, cite specific situations. Do not fall into the trap. Explain what you can and then observe the following:

1. Remind him that the truth may hurt.
2. The truth may be the other person's perception.
3. Perceptions count.
4. There may be something of value to learn about himself from the perception.
5. You will want to be on his team to help make a difference.

Many CEO's, presidents, administrative assistants, technical aids, supervisors, or human resource professionals become the enabler to the difficult employee. When you give critical feedback or plan an intervention, you will want to be compassionate. But, do not enable the behavior to go on and on without some change in attitude or insight.

If you have become the agent or sponsor of these changes and you are spending more energy on it than the identified problem person, or if you are the only one committed to the desired changes, you have lost your position as an appropriate mentor or interventionist.

If you are afraid of the outburst, retribution in any form, tell the difficult person exactly what you are afraid of. Then remind him or her that your intention to work together for a very long time, and the feedback you are giving is in the interest of that long working relationship. *Tough love* works on the job.

Last, you will sleep well if you do plant the seed. Perhaps the change will come slowly. Perhaps you will not benefit directly from the intervention. Perhaps you will take a little heat yourself from the perplexed employee. Sometimes you may have been the very first person to give the information as directly as you have. Sometimes you are the last straw for the person who has heard the feedback all his life, and you have broken his back with the news...

1. You, too, are only a human being.
2. Do the best you can.
3. Be prepared to talk again.
4. Have your own support team ready to comfort you.
5. Appreciate your courage.
6. Remember that some day, he or she may also appreciate it!

Good luck in your search for **Red Inkers**. Remember the point is just to find a way to justify the cost of training. Without training, these employees cost a lot anyway.

Warning: GLC programs are also offered to black ink high potential employees who have no major flaws and simply need leadership enhancement programs.

Appendix

The GLC Leadership Programs:

We explore each person's blind spots and help them to get a new focus on what goes wrong for them, no matter how well intentioned those behaviors seem to be. We seek out belief systems about their behavior which may have worked in the eighth grade, maybe even as an professor's aid in college, and maybe even in their first job.

When their shiny faces and diplomas and brains took on the world, they were without the scar tissue build-up and without the opportunity to burn a bridge which was not yet built. Eventually, however, the bad habits caused from faulty or antiquated belief systems, take their toll.

We've learned about what works and what doesn't. We've learned what working styles are antithetical to their tasks and their colleagues. We've learned the ways they learn and what ways they teach. We meet with the managers, sometimes sympathetically, often with healthy confrontation—always with the realities in mind, so our employee participant can start breathing well again.

We've also learned how much money they earn, their peers earn, their managers earn. All of this is pretty private in many companies, but we still learn it all, from employees suffering from the inequities or the fears of not earning their own keep. So we had a lot of data with which to work. We even talked to the subordinates who shared how much time and angst they spent stressing about an inadequate boss.

We learned that peers were often affected by their own power-lessness or control issues or fears of sabotage. We learned that an intimidator can drain the intellectual guts right out of a colleague. Or a withholder can suck out the creativity of a peer when he continues to bump his head against the wall for information or cooperation. We learned that trust is fragile, and fighting for it is a serious war—not a battle. We learned that the dysfunctional employee can't help it. He is sometimes trained or created by his environment and sometimes becomes the scapegoat to his organization.

But more times than that, we learned that the problem em-ployee is often his own worst enemy. He invites havoc and mayhem whenever he opens wide or tightly shuts his lips. He could be so much more productive if he were shown when to speak up and when not to. Our participants actually find out about their impact on others, and that what they say and how they say it can make the difference in their career.

The following is from a document we present to our clients so that they can assess our company:

How is GLC Different From Other Companies?

1. We do 80% results-oriented interventions and only 20% assessment.
2. We have developed a tool to estimate the cost of the difficult executive.
3. We work with 5 company goals, 5 employee goals, and achieve results!
4. We offer real time on-the-job tools and techniques.
5. We give complete feedback by combining confron-tation with support.

6. We have both business and behavioral science back grounds.
7. We use multiple coaches to better mirror real life `situations.
8. We offer mentoring groups with previously graduated executives.
9. We facilitate real time conflict resolution at the company.
10. We role-play the new behavior and give immediate feedback!
11. We teach how to make it obvious to others too!
12. We teach the value of seeking feedback to anchor the changes.
13. We get deeply, seriously, passionately involved in the results!
14. We do maintenance, not just a 2 day off-site class and forget it.
15. We work at your office or our own facility...
16. We are local—Mountain View, near 85, 237, & 101

How is GLC the Same as Other Coaching Companies?

1. We use video, audio, homework, management confer ences.
2. We involve managers, HR persons, or any referrals, and prepare reports.
3. We use 360s, yours or ours, and appraisal reviews.
4. We have a very experienced staff!

For more information about our study and further work in this field, you may call or write for a White Paper: Growth & Leadership Center, 1451 Grant Road, Mountain View, California, 94040. Phone (415) 966-1144, Fax (415) 966-1609, Email: //HTTP:www.glc-corp.com.

<u>WARNING:</u> GLC PROGRAMS ARE ALSO OFFERED TO BLACK INK HIGH POTENTIAL EMPLOYEES WHO HAVE NO MAJOR FLAWS AND SIMPLY NEED LEADERSHIP ENHANCEMENT PROGRAMS.

GLC Red Ink Behavior -   Costimator Analysis

DATA COLLECTION
We begin the analysis with data. These will be approximations and/or best guesses. In the case of peers and subordinates, e.g., their salary, indicate what you feel is a reasonable average.

Please supply the following information:

* Include all benefits in salaries (e.g., stocks, bonuses, insurances, etc...)

Last:		First:		Company	
Title:					
Problem Description:					

Salary ($K/yr)*:		Severance package ($K):	
DEP's lost hours/week:		Search hiring ($K):	
Problem duration (Mo):		Training ($K):	

Manager's sal ($K/yr)*:		HR person's sal ($K/yr)*:	
Manager's lost hrs/wk:		HR person's lost hrs/wk:	
Dur.of intervention (Mo):		Other persons ($K/wk):	

Number of peers:		Number of subordinates:	
Peers' salary ($K/yr)*:		Subordinates' salary ($K/yr)*:	
Peers' lost hrs/wk:		Subordinates' lost hrs/wk:	

Revenues responsibilities ($K)		GLC program cost ($K):	
Loss on revenues (%):		GLC program duration (hrs):	
		Opportunity cost to company (%):	

GLC Red Ink Behavior - Costimator Analysis

Please supply the following information:

ID: 59

* Include all benefits in salaries (e.g., stocks, bonuses, insurances, etc...)

Last: X	First: X	Company X
Title:	Dir. Marketing	
Problem Description:	Do it yourself. Hard working, conscientious. VP promotable. Hightech interest, low mgt interest.	

Salary ($K/yr)*:	120	Severance package ($K):	120
DEP's lost hours/week:	2	Search hiring ($K):	45
Problem duration (Mo):	12	Training ($K):	60
Direct Cost:	**$6,000**	**Replacement Cost:**	**$225,000**

Manager's sal ($K/yr)*:	200	HR person's sal ($K/yr)*:	100
Manager's lost hrs/wk:	0.25	HR person's lost hrs/wk:	0.25
Dur.of intervention (Mo):	3	Other persons ($K/wk):	0
	Intervention Cost:		**$469**

Number of peers:	3	Number of subordinates:	6
Peers' salary ($K/yr)*:	120	Subordinates' salary ($K/yr)*:	80
Peers' lost hrs/wk:	2	Subordinates' lost hrs/wk:	2
	Impact Cost (People):		**$42,000**

Revenues responsibilities ($K)	3000	GLC program cost ($K):	12
Loss on revenues (%):	2	GLC program duration (hrs):	25
		Opportunity cost to company (%):	7
Impact Cost (Revenues):	**$60,000**	**GLC Program Total Cost:**	**$13,672**

Sunk Cost ($):	**$108,469**	**Replacement Cost:**	**$225,000**
Burn Rate ($/Mo)	**$9,156**	**Payback (Mo):**	**1.5**

GLC Red Ink Behavior - Costimator Analysis

| Please supply the following information: | | ID: | 64 |

* Include all benefits in salaries (e.g., stocks, bonuses, insurances, etc...)

| Last: | X | First: | X | Company | X |

| Title: | Medical Doc., Research VP |
| Problem Description: | Intimidates, critical, belitting, impulsive, does not delegate, procrastinates |

Salary ($K/yr)*:	150	Severance package ($K):	70
DEP's lost hours/week:	2	Search hiring ($K):	30
Problem duration (Mo):	6	Training ($K):	12
Direct Cost:	**$3,750**	**Replacement Cost:**	**$112,000**

Manager's sal ($K/yr)*:	300	HR person's sal ($K/yr)*:	50
Manager's lost hrs/wk:	2	HR person's lost hrs/wk:	1
Dur.of intervention (Mo):	6	Other persons ($K/wk):	0
	Intervention Cost:	**$8,125**	

Number of peers:	5	Number of subordinates:	6
Peers' salary ($K/yr)*:	200	Subordinates' salary ($K/yr)*:	65
Peers' lost hrs/wk:	2	Subordinates' lost hrs/wk:	4
	Impact Cost (People):	**$44,500**	

Revenues responsibilities ($K)	800	GLC program cost ($K):	12
Loss on revenues (%):	5	GLC program duration (hrs):	15
		Opportunity cost to company (%):	2
Impact Cost (Revenues):	**$20,000**	**GLC Program Total Cost:**	**$13,195**

Sunk Cost ($):	**$76,375**	**Replacement Cost:**	**$112,000**
Burn Rate ($/Mo)	**$12,729**	**Payback (Mo):**	**1.0**

GLC Red Ink Behavior - Costimator Analysis

Please supply the following information: | ID: | 62 |

* Include all benefits in salaries (e.g., stocks, bonuses, insurances, etc...)

Last:	X	First:	X		Company	X
Title:	Controller					
Problem Description:	Victimized, ineffective, not a leader					

Salary ($K/yr)*:	500	Severance package ($K):	600
DEP's lost hours/week:	3	Search hiring ($K):	200
Problem duration (Mo):	36	Training ($K):	150
Direct Cost:	**$112,500**	**Replacement Cost:**	**$950,000**

Manager's sal ($K/yr)*:	1000	HR person's sal ($K/yr)*:	80
Manager's lost hrs/wk:	1	HR person's lost hrs/wk:	1
Dur.of intervention (Mo):	12	Other persons ($K/wk):	0
	Intervention Cost:	**$27,000**	

Number of peers:	10	Number of subordinates:	4
Peers' salary ($K/yr)*:	500	Subordinates' salary ($K/yr)*:	100
Peers' lost hrs/wk:	1	Subordinates' lost hrs/wk:	4
	Impact Cost (People):	**$495,000**	

Revenues responsibilities ($K)	2000	GLC program cost ($K):	40
Loss on revenues (%):	2	GLC program duration (hrs):	36
		Opportunity cost to company (%):	5
Impact Cost (Revenues):	**$120,000**	**GLC Program Total Cost:**	**$49,844**

Sunk Cost ($):	**$754,500**	**Replacement Cost:**	**$950,000**
Burn Rate ($/Mo)	**$22,458**	**Payback (Mo):**	**2.2**

GLC Red Ink Behavior - Costimator Analysis

| Please supply the following information: | ID: | 60 |

* Include all benefits in salaries (e.g., stocks, bonuses, insurances, etc...)

| Last: | X | First: | X | Company | X |

| Title: | Dir. Eng. |
| Problem Description: | Intimidator, sarcastic. Sexual harassment claims. Good guy. |

Salary ($K/yr)*:	80	Severance package ($K):	80
DEP's lost hours/week:	2	Search hiring ($K):	20
Problem duration (Mo):	12	Training ($K):	20
Direct Cost:	**$4,000**	**Replacement Cost:**	**$120,000**

Manager's sal ($K/yr)*:	150	HR person's sal ($K/yr)*:	150
Manager's lost hrs/wk:	0.66	HR person's lost hrs/wk:	1
Dur.of intervention (Mo):	3	Other persons ($K/wk):	0
Intervention Cost:		**$1,556**	

Number of peers:	5	Number of subordinates:	8
Peers' salary ($K/yr)*:	80	Subordinates' salary ($K/yr)*:	60
Peers' lost hrs/wk:	2	Subordinates' lost hrs/wk:	2
Impact Cost (People):		**$44,000**	

Revenues responsibilities ($K)	500	GLC program cost ($K):	9
Loss on revenues (%):	2	GLC program duration (hrs):	15
		Opportunity cost to company (%):	5
Impact Cost (Revenues):	**$10,000**	**GLC Program Total Cost:**	**$9,656**

| **Sunk Cost ($):** | **$59,556** | **Replacement Cost:** | **$120,000** |
| **Burn Rate ($/Mo)** | **$5,352** | **Payback (Mo):** | **1.8** |

GLC Red Ink Behavior - Costimator Analysis

Please supply the following information:	ID:	63

* Include all benefits in salaries (e.g., stocks, bonuses, insurances, etc...)

Last: X	First: X	Company X
Title:	VP, Finance	
Problem Description:	Grooming for presidency	

Salary ($K/yr)*:	500	Severance package ($K):	500
DEP's lost hours/week:	2	Search hiring ($K):	100
Problem duration (Mo):	12	Training ($K):	150
Direct Cost:	**$25,000**	**Replacement Cost:**	**$750,000**

Manager's sal ($K/yr)*:	1000	HR person's sal ($K/yr)*:	65
Manager's lost hrs/wk:	0.25	HR person's lost hrs/wk:	1
Dur. of intervention (Mo):	6	Other persons ($K/wk):	15
	Intervention Cost:	**$4,298**	

Number of peers:	14	Number of subordinates:	10
Peers' salary ($K/yr)*:	200	Subordinates' salary ($K/yr)*:	100
Peers' lost hrs/wk:	2	Subordinates' lost hrs/wk:	2
	Impact Cost (People):	**$190,000**	

Revenues responsibilities ($K)	2000	GLC program cost ($K):	14.99
Loss on revenues (%):	10	GLC program duration (hrs):	25
		Opportunity cost to company (%):	15
Impact Cost (Revenues):	**$200,000**	**GLC Program Total Cost:**	**$22,474**

Sunk Cost ($):	**$418,938**	**Replacement Cost:**	**$750,000**
Burn Rate ($/Mo)	**$35,240**	**Payback (Mo):**	**0.6**

GLC Red Ink Behavior - Costimator Analysis

Please supply the following information:		ID:	65

* Include all benefits in salaries (e.g., stocks, bonuses, insurances, etc...)

Last:	X	First:	X	Company	X
Title:	VP, Finance				
Problem Description:	Abusive, intimidating				

Salary ($K/yr)*:	1000	Severance package ($K):	2000
DEP's lost hours/week:	10	Search hiring ($K):	150
Problem duration (Mo):	12	Training ($K):	350
Direct Cost:	**$250,000**	**Replacement Cost:**	**$2,500,000**

Manager's sal ($K/yr)*:	2000	HR person's sal ($K/yr)*:	0
Manager's lost hrs/wk:	0.25	HR person's lost hrs/wk:	0
Dur.of intervention (Mo):	12	Other persons ($K/wk):	0
	Intervention Cost:	**$12,500**	

Number of peers:	0	Number of subordinates:	12
Peers' salary ($K/yr)*:	0	Subordinates' salary ($K/yr)*:	100
Peers' lost hrs/wk:	0	Subordinates' lost hrs/wk:	1
	Impact Cost (People):	**$30,000**	

Revenues responsibilities ($K)	9000	GLC program cost ($K):	15
Loss on revenues (%):	5	GLC program duration (hrs):	30
		Opportunity cost to company (%):	5
Impact Cost (Revenues):	**$450,000**	**GLC Program Total Cost:**	**$31,406**

Sunk Cost ($):	**$742,500**	**Replacement Cost:**	**$2,500,000**
Burn Rate ($/Mo)	**$61,875**	**Payback (Mo):**	**0.5**

Red Ink Behaviors

The following table represents our original model of the Costimator:

Item	Description
Direct Cost	
Number of people involved (#)	Number of people directly incapacitated during the time, including the major player (This model assumes all these people have the same salary)
Yearly salary (including benefits)	
Salary ($/hr, including benefits)	Hourly salary of the major player(s). If you have only the yearly salary, divide by 1,800. Remember to include benefits, bonuses, etc...
Opportunity cost ($/hr)	Evaluation of the loss of benefit to the company per work hour the major player(s) was(were) out of commission (Mgrs = $0)
Unproductive time (hrs/wk)	Number of hours per week during which the major player(s) becomes unproductive (venting, absent, complaining, etc...)
Duration of conflict (wks)	Time in weeks the problem has been occurring or might occur (45 weeks to estimate a yearly cost)
Intervention Cost	
Yearly salary (Including benefits)	
Mgr salary ($/hr, including benefits)	Hourly salary of one mediator. If you have only the yearly salary, divide by 1,800. Remember to include benefits, bonuses, etc...
Number of mgrs involved (#)	Number of managers directly involved during the time , including the major player (This model assumes all these managers have the same salary)
Unproductive time (hrs/wk/mgr)	Number of hours per week during which the mgrs becomes unproductive while dealing with the problem (consulting, mediating, writing letters, etc...)
Duration of intervention (wks)	Time in weeks the intervention has been or will be in place (45 weeks to estimate a yearly cost)
Inappropriate solution ($)	Loss consequent to trying to implement the wrong solution (Internal backfire, etc...)
Replacement Cost	(Use this section only if the decision is made)
Severance package ($)	Estimate of the package to be payed to the major player to leave the Co.
Vacant position ($)	Estimate of the cost of leaving the major player's position vacant for a while
Search ($)	Estimate of the total search cost to fill the major player's position
Hiring ($)	Estimate of the total hiring cost for the major player's position
Training ($)	Estimate of the total training cost for the major player's position

Sphere of Influence Cost

Sphere of influence (# people)	Number of people impacted by or suffering from the problem described above, but not directly involved in it nor in its remedy
Team member salary ($/hr)	Their hourly salary (average per person). If you have only the yearly salary, divide by 1,800. Remember to include benefits, bonuses, etc...
Morale decay	Estimate in percents of the decrease in morale as a consequence of the problem
Poor role modeling	Estimate in percents of the decrease in role modeling as a consequence of the problem
Loss of creativity	Estimate in percents of the decrease in creativity (= freedom to think, fear to say something stupid) as a consequence of the problem
Loss of productivity	Estimate in percents of the decrease in productivity (fear to make mistakes, low motivation) as a consequence of the problem

Impact on Revenues

Revenues (Products & contracts)	Total amount of revenues the major player is supposed to generate or to control per year
Loss on revenues (%)	Estimate of the loss in percents on these revenues as a consequence of the problem (delays, penalty, loss of contract, loss of clients)

Total Cost

% of major player's salary	
Burning Rate ($/week)	
Suggested Program	Program which could remedy (or prevent) the situation
Out-of-pocket program cost	Program total cost
Time spent in the program (hrs)	Total number of hours the major player(s) will spend out of the company to attend the program (Include commute)
Opportunity cost to Co. (%)	Percents of hourly salary the Co. loses from the major player(s) attending the program
Indirect program cost	
Total program cost	
Total amount saved	
Return on investment ($ per $1)	($# saved per $1 invested)
Pay-back time (months)	
Total amount saved	

LEADERSHIP DEVELOPMENT PROFILE

Participant's Name:_____ Title:_____ ID #:___ Date:___/___/___

You are his/her: Manager ___ Peer ___ Subordinate ___ Other (What?) _____

Note: Circle your choice. If you encounter a question that you feel unqualified to answer, circle the "?".

YOUR ASSESSMENT OF...

Participant's Overall Characteristics

	Lo				Hi	
Visionary / Strategic Thinker	1	2	3	4	5	?
Innovative	1	2	3	4	5	?
Keeps commitments	1	2	3	4	5	?
Customer Orientation	1	2	3	4	5	?
Of High Character	1	2	3	4	5	?
Supportive of Others	1	2	3	4	5	?
Collaborative	1	2	3	4	5	?
Works to Benefit Company	1	2	3	4	5	?
Non-defensive	1	2	3	4	5	?
Reacts well to criticism	1	2	3	4	5	?
Genuine / Non-Manipulative	1	2	3	4	5	?
Manages Time & Priorities	1	2	3	4	5	?
Effective use of humor	1	2	3	4	5	?

Relationship with His/Her Manager

	Lo				Hi	
Keeps commitments	1	2	3	4	5	?
Manager's Success Is Important	1	2	3	4	5	?
Trustworthy	1	2	3	4	5	?
Willing to Challenge	1	2	3	4	5	?
Supports After Losing	1	2	3	4	5	?
Influences Manager's Thinking	1	2	3	4	5	?
Meets due dates	1	2	3	4	5	?
Focused on Making Goals	1	2	3	4	5	?
Takes Critical Feedback Well	1	2	3	4	5	?
Gives Critical Feedback Well	1	2	3	4	5	?
Adaptable to Change	1	2	3	4	5	?
Takes Responsibility for Errors	1	2	3	4	5	?
Exhibits Competency	1	2	3	4	5	?

Relationship with Subordinates

	Lo				Hi	
Leadership Effectiveness	1	2	3	4	5	?
Sets Clear Expectations	1	2	3	4	5	?
Measures Results	1	2	3	4	5	?
Sets Clear Consequences	1	2	3	4	5	?
Delegates well	1	2	3	4	5	?
Trustworthy	1	2	3	4	5	?
Supportive When Asked	1	2	3	4	5	?
Subordinate Success Important	1	2	3	4	5	?
Good Coaching Skills	1	2	3	4	5	?
Takes Critical Feedback Well	1	2	3	4	5	?
Gives Critical Feedback Well	1	2	3	4	5	?
Listens Well	1	2	3	4	5	?
Empowers Initiative	1	2	3	4	5	?
Promotes Collaboration	1	2	3	4	5	?
Realistic Expectations	1	2	3	4	5	?
Does not *Micromanage*	1	2	3	4	5	?

Relationship with Peers

	Lo				Hi	
Influences Peers	1	2	3	4	5	?
Doesn't Control/Intimidate	1	2	3	4	5	?
Fully participative	1	2	3	4	5	?
Team-oriented	1	2	3	4	5	?
Trustworthy	1	2	3	4	5	?
Exhibits competency	1	2	3	4	5	?
Collaborative	1	2	3	4	5	?
Appreciates differing inputs	1	2	3	4	5	?
Takes Critical Feedback Well	1	2	3	4	5	?
Gives Critical Feedback Well	1	2	3	4	5	?
Adaptable to New Ideas	1	2	3	4	5	?
Respects Differing Views	1	2	3	4	5	?

Comments: _____

_____

_____